Cooking Recipe

MW01674701

Make the Best Grilled Meals for Your Family and Friends

By

Marlow Strickland

Table of Contents

Introduction

Pit Boss Wood Pellet Smoker Grill is one of our newest outdoor grills and smoker combos. It has it all: the ultimate cooking environment, a compact footprint, and an unbeatable price. Its ability to smoke and grill is unmatched, with the capacity to grill for up to 700 guests. So if you've been looking for the perfect smoker/grill combo but could not find one that had all the features you wanted, search no more.

Pit Boss Wood Pellet Smoker Grill has many features that make it stand out from other models on our site.

This grill is the best value you can find on the market for a smoking and grilling combo. It's perfect for those who need space or budget constraints. Pit Boss has two side shelves that fold up when not in use, leaving more space to cook when needed. It also has a fold-down warming rack, so you can cook more without having to open up your pit early. You can put it on the side of your house or in your garage and still have plenty of room to store other things.

Pit Boss is also a multi-fuel grill, meaning you can switch from wood to charcoal in under 10 minutes. It comes with everything you need to start smoking right out of the box. You don't have to worry about temperatures or knowing which wood pellets work best for certain kinds of meat, like other wood pellet smokers. That's because Pit Boss comes with their patented cook control system that lets you set precise temperature thresholds and wood pellet ratios for your grilling needs.

Pit Boss has a large 640 sq. in. total cooking area and an additional 640 sq. in. warming rack, in addition to thick, double-walled legs that are specifically designed for outdoor cooking. The thick stainless steel walls are durable and strong enough to withstand the harshest conditions and use while still looking great at your home or cabin! The legs have a channeled bottom for safe smoking under any weather conditions, including rain or snow.

The front and top racks of this grill provide you with a total of 680 sq. in. of cooking space! That is very close to the 700 sq. in.

Structure

Pit Boss Wood Pellet Smoker Grill looks great in any outdoor setting. The stainless steel legs and double-walled body also have an attractive black powder-coated steel hood with a grease cup. Because this is a wood pellet smoker, it can smoke well over 10 hours at a time without adding more fuel. It also has one of the most durable, high-quality knobs on the market.

Smoking

When you're ready to start smoking, Pit Boss will provide you with more than enough power for your grilling needs. It boasts an impressive 2,500 sq. in. cooking space, including two 675 sq. in. cooking grates and two upper and lower vents, letting you smoke for up to 4 hours at a time!

It also gives you a total of 13 pre-set temperature settings that you can easily adjust to your needs. This grill has an automatic self-cleaning feature, so your cooking space will always be ready for another cookout! You'll also be able to monitor the internal temperature of your food with the thermometer on the door.

There are many grilling accessories available that can make your Pit Boss Wood Pellet Smoker Grill even more versatile and useful, without all the extra expense of buying separate tools or accessories.

Money and Time Saver

The tool you need to save money and time is right here!

No need to spend money on expensive wood pellets when these will last longer than you can imagine. No need to spend time chopping wood or looking for the right kind of wood. These are easy to use, durable, and affordable in comparison to other types of pellets. You won't be going back to charcoal anytime soon after using these! :)

From start to finish, your grill is ready for cooking! The filter cup makes filling and cleaning the hopper a breeze, and since it holds up to a full 60 lbs. of pellets at once, you won't have to worry about running out in the middle of grilling season.

Pit Boss offers a frying pan accessory for this grill, which you can add to your package for an amazing price of $19.99 - that means you already have a grill and a smoker! This frying pan is made from cast iron to make sure that whatever you fry stays crisp and delicious. It also comes with a convenient drain hole at the bottom of the pan to help collect unwanted grease for easy disposal.

No need for firewood

You can use this independently, without firewood. All the fuel you need is contained within the grill.

This grill saves energy costs because there is no need for added gas or charcoal. The only thing you have to do is to plug it in

When you are hosting a party, this is a good alternative to the traditional grills. It can cook a larger quantity of food, save time and money by not having a long cooking session.

Easy to clean

Just wipe the grease and use soap for a quick clean. You can have it as clean as new in minutes.

This is the best feature of this grill. It has heavy-duty mesh, which allows for an easier cleaning process.

It does not rust either. Stainless steel grill is a good alternative to stainless steel appliances, and it will last longer because of the heavy-duty mesh.

No stress on your back

Since you need to do nothing but walk away while the greasewood pellet cooker cooks your food, you can spend more time socializing or doing other things without worrying about firewood or gas grill running out of fuel or charcoal as these tend to happen quite frequently, especially if you are hosting a barbecue party with a traditional charcoal or gas grill at your home. This high-efficiency pellet wood smoke cooker takes care of all these problems.

You don't have to buy firewood which saves you money over time. They can last for years, and you can be assured of consistent heat. It is easy to maintain, and on top of all that, it doesn't require much skill to use. This grill will save you a lot of trouble during those busy summer nights when your friends are over, allowing you more time with them

If anything is holding back this grill from being perfect, It's the size.

Cook like a chef and impress them

The Pit Boss Wood Pellet Smoker Grill will allow you to smoke, grill, and bake with the best cooking tools available. You will be able to easily make the perfect barbecue meats, deliciously done fish and seafood, and so much more!

Get everything you need in one unit. The Pit Boss Wood Pellet Smoker Grill has all of your smoking needs covered with plenty of room for grilling when not in use.

Have friends over or corporate events at your place? The large cooking area on this smoker grill makes it easy to cook a larger quantity of food at one time. No more "scrounging around," looking for a place on your outdoor grill to make extra food. You can cook your main dish and sides simultaneously, with no extra effort on your part. This saves you time and money!

No need to worry about the weather conditions while you're cooking. The Pit Boss Wood Pellet Smoker Grill is built from durable materials that will withstand all types of weather conditions so that you can enjoy grilling and smoking no matter what Mother Nature throws your way.

Everything needed in one unit Extra large cooking area for main dishes, sides, extras Large capacity holds up to 60 lbs.

Get the same results using less wood. The Pit Boss Wood Pellet Smoker Grill has an adjustable air control system that allows you to control the air intake and help regulate how much wood is going through the unit at one time. This controls how much heat you put out, as well as how many pellets are going through the unit at any given time, saving you money and helping you get a great smoke flavor!

Besides, the bottom warming rack holds up to 20 lbs of food, great for entertaining. The fold-down warming rack is great when cooking large items like whole chickens or fish.

Impress them with the perfect BBQ grilling recipe for your family, friends, or co-workers. Our Pit Boss Wood Pellet Grill is the ultimate easy-to-use outdoor cooking grill that will deliver your food with unparalleled convenience and flavour.

Our smart grill is loaded with high-tech features that help you get the precise results you want. The built-in meat probe and side shelf allow all of your food to be cooked evenly without babysitting the grill; the food sensor display lets you know when your meat has reached its internal temperature. These great features combine to make grilling even easier.

The single most important aspect of a BBQ grill when cooking outdoors is efficiency – your fuel should last as long as possible to reduce time spent refuelling and clean-up between cooks. That's why Pit Boss designed our pit grill to burn wood pellets as fuel, eliminating the need for messy propane canisters.

You'll also love the starter set, designed to provide you with everything you need to start grilling immediately. The 36" x 18" cast iron cooking grates are heavy and made of premium materials, while the side shelves are a convenient spot for your hot coals and grill tools. The cast iron drip pan is perfect for collecting drippings and leftovers.

Unlike most pellet grills on the market, our Pit Boss wood pellet grill uses one of the finest available wood-burning grills. We use only premium quality hardwood to create a combustion chamber where high-quality pellets burn cleanly and efficiently. Besides, we use specialized venturi-assisted opening valves that supplement airflow, making your food taste even better when cooked on our pit grill.

How to Use Your Pit Boss Wood Pellet Grill?

Pellet grills are high-tech machines that are powered by a motor connected to an auger system, where wood pellets are dropped into an enclosed area and then distributed evenly over hot coals. A digital controller regulates temperature by turning the drill on or off as necessary to maintain steady temperatures throughout the cooking process. A thermostat attached to the drill regulates the final temperature. Propane and charcoal are also delivered through a tube into a chamber to supply additional heat. A hopper on top of the drill delivers pellets when needed. The standard drill operates at a maximum speed of about 200 to 210 pounds per hour at temps between 180 and 200 degrees, depending on the type of pellets used.

This grill is easy to use, easy to clean up, and looks great. It comes with a large cooking area and a hopper that feeds the pellets into the grill continuously. The best part about using this grill is that you do not need to mess with any gas or charcoal because there is no open flame. You just plug it in, turn it on, and let it cook.

The Pit Boss 700 also comes with a meat probe that measures its temperature while it cooks. This feature allows you to leave once you are done cooking, so you don't have to sacrifice time to sit there and watch your food cook.

The benefit of using wood pellets is that they do not have smoke points, or what is commonly referred to as juiciness, leading to more even cooking temperatures and fewer flare-ups at all times during the smoking process. The low smoke point also makes them ideal for cooking with smaller amounts of meat because it will take longer for your meat to be fully cooked before it burns and tastes burnt.

The top of the grill has a pan for grilling and an assortment of cooking racks. It comes with one oil drip pan, and a grease drip pan placed just below the cooking grates. There is also a drip tray above the grease drip pan. That brings me to the next benefit of this grill, the grease container located on top of your food inside the grill. This eliminates all that excess grease that normally builds up around the edges because now your food will not sit in it. The flavor from all those juices will also be retained due to this grill's large cooking area, which keeps your meat tasting fresh and well-seasoned rather than dry and crunchy (which is what happens when cooking over direct heat).

Vegetable Recipes

1. Roasted Fall Vegetables

Preparation Time: 10 minutes

Cooking Time: 35 minutes

Servings: 8

Ingredients:

- Potatoes – ½ pound
- Brussels sprouts, halved – ½ pound
- Butternut squash, dice – ½ pound
- Cremini mushrooms, halved – 1 pint
- Salt – 1 tablespoon
- Ground black pepper – ¾ tablespoon

- Olive oil – 2 tablespoons

Directions:

1. In the meantime, take a large bowl, place potatoes in it, add salt and black pepper, drizzle with oil and then toss until coated.
2. Take a sheet tray and then spread seasoned potatoes on it.
3. When the grill has preheated, place a sheet pan containing potatoes on the grilling rack and then grill for 15 minutes.
4. Then add mushrooms, sprouts into the pan, toss to coat, and then continue grilling for 20 minutes until all the vegetables have turned nicely browned and thoroughly cooked.
5. Serve immediately.

Nutrition:

- Calories: 80 Carbs: 7g
- Fat: 6g Protein: 1g

2. Roasted Pumpkin Seeds

Preparation Time: 10 minutes

Cooking Time: 40 minutes

Servings: 8

Ingredients:

Pumpkin seeds – 1 pound

Salt – 1 tablespoon

Olive oil – 1 tablespoon

Directions:

1. In the meantime, take a baking sheet, grease it with oil, spread pumpkin seeds on it and then stir until coated.
2. When the grill has preheated, place a baking sheet containing pumpkin on the grilling rack and let grill for 20 minutes.
3. Season pumpkin seeds with salt, switch the grill temperature to 325 degrees F and continue grilling for 20 minutes until roasted.
4. When done, let pumpkin seeds cool slightly and then serve.

Nutrition:

- Calories: 130
- Carbs: 13g
- Fat: 5g
- Protein 8g

3. Wood Pellet Cold Smoked Cheese

Preparation Time: 5 minutes

Cooking Time: 2 minutes

Servings: 10

Ingredients:

- Ice
- One aluminum pan, full-size and disposable
- One aluminum pan, half-size, and disposable
- Toothpicks
- A block of cheese

Directions:

1. Preheat the wood pellet to 165°F with the lid closed for 15 minutes.
2. Place the small pan in the large pan. Fill the surrounding of the small pan with ice.
3. Place the cheese in the small pan on top of toothpicks, then place the pan on the grill and close the lid.
4. Smoke cheese for 1 hour, flip the cheese, and smoke for one more hour with the lid closed.

5. Remove the cheese from the grill and wrap it in parchment paper. Store in the fridge for 2 3 days for the smoke flavor to mellow.
6. Remove from the fridge and serve. Enjoy.

Nutrition:

Calories: 1910

Total Fat: 7g

Saturated Fat: 6g

Total Carbs: 2g

Net Carbs: 2g

Protein: 6g

Sugar: 1g

Fiber: 0g

Sodium: 340mg

Potassium: 0mg

4. Wood Pellet Smoked Asparagus

Preparation Time: 5 minutes

Cooking Time: 1 hour

Servings: 4

Ingredients:

- One bunch of fresh asparagus ends cut
- 2 tbsp. olive oil
- Salt and pepper to taste

Directions:

1. Fire up your wood pellet smoker to 230°F
2. Place the asparagus in a mixing bowl and drizzle with olive oil. Season with salt and pepper.
3. Place the asparagus in a tinfoil sheet and fold the sides such that you create a basket.
4. Smoke the asparagus for 1 hour or until soft, turning after half an hour.
5. Remove from the grill and serve. Enjoy.

Nutrition:

Calories: 43

Total Fat: 2g

Total Carbs: 4g

Net Carbs: 2g

Protein: 3g

Sugar: 2g

Fiber: 2g

Sodium: 148mg

5. Wood Pellet Grilled Mexican Street Corn

Preparation Time: 5 minutes

Cooking Time: 25 minutes

Servings: 6

Ingredients:

- Six ears of corn on the cob
- 1 tbsp. olive oil
- Kosher salt and pepper to taste
- 1/4 cup mayo
- 1/4 cup sour cream
- 1 tbsp. garlic paste

- 1/2 tbsp. chili powder
- Pinch of ground red pepper
- 1/2 cup coria cheese, crumbled
- 1/4 cup cilantro, chopped
- Six lime wedges

Directions:

1. Brush the corn with oil.
2. Sprinkle with salt.
3. Place the corn on a wood pellet grill set at 350°F. Cook for 25 minutes as you turn it occasionally.
4. Meanwhile, mix mayo, cream, garlic, chili, and red pepper until well combined.
5. Let it rest for some minutes, then brush with the mayo mixture.
6. Sprinkle cottage cheese, more chili powder, and cilantro. Serve with lime wedges. Enjoy.

Nutrition:

Calories: 144

Total Fat: 5g

Saturated Fat: 2g

Total Carbs: 10g

Net Carbs: 10g

Protein: 0g

Sugar: 0g

Fiber: 0g

Sodium: 136mg

Potassium: 173mg

6. Crispy Garlic Potatoes

Preparation Time: 15 minutes

Cooking Time: 40 minutes

Servings: 4

Ingredients:

- Baby potatoes, scrubbed – 1 pound

- Large white onion, peeled, sliced - 1
- Garlic, peeled, sliced - 3
- Chopped parsley - 1 teaspoon
- Butter, unsalted, sliced - 3 tablespoons

Directions:

1. In the meantime, cut potatoes in slices and then arrange them on a large piece of foil or baking sheet, separating potatoes by onion slices and butter.
2. Sprinkle garlic slices over vegetables, and then season with salt, black pepper, and parsley.
3. When the grill has preheated, place a baking sheet containing potato mixture on the grilling rack and grill for 40 minutes until potato slices have turned tender.
4. Serve immediately.

Nutrition:

- Calories: 150
- Carbs: 15g
- Fat: 10g
- Protein: 1g

7. Grilled Corn With Honey Butter

Servings: 6

Cooking Time: 10 Minutes

Ingredients:

- 6 pieces corn, husked
- 2 tablespoons olive oil
- Salt and pepper to taste
- ½ cup butter, room temperature
- ½ cup honey

Directions:

1. Fire the grill to 350F. Use desired wood pellets when cooking. Close the lid and preheat for 15 minutes.
2. Brush the corn with oil and season with salt and pepper to taste.
3. Place the corn on the grill grate and cook for 10 minutes. Make sure to flip the corn halfway through the cooking time for even cooking.
4. Meanwhile, mix the butter and honey in a small bowl. Set aside.
5. Once the corn is cooked, remove it from the grill and brush it with the honey butter sauce.

Nutrition Info: Calories per serving: 387; Protein: 5g; Carbs: 51.2g; Fat: 21.6g Sugar: 28.2g

8. Roasted Parmesan Cheese Broccoli

Servings: 3 To 4

Cooking Time: 45 Minutes

Ingredients:

- 3cups broccoli stems trimmed
- 1tbsp lemon juice
- 1tbsp olive oil
- 2garlic cloves, minced
- 1/2 tsp kosher salt
- 1/2 tsp ground black pepper
- 1tsp lemon zest
- 1/8 cup parmesan cheese, grated

Directions:

1. Preheat pellet grill to 375°F.
2. Place broccoli in a resealable bag. Add lemon juice, olive oil, garlic cloves, salt, and pepper. Seal the bag and toss to combine. Let the mixture marinate for 30 minutes.
3. Pour broccoli into a grill basket. Place basket on grill grates to roast. Grill broccoli for 14-18 minutes, flipping broccoli halfway through. Grill until tender yet a little crispy on the outside.
4. Remove broccoli from grill and place on a serving dish—zest with lemon and top with grated parmesan cheese. Serve immediately and enjoy!

Nutrition Info: Calories: 82.6 Fat: 4.6 g Cholesterol: 1.8 mg Carbohydrate: 8.1 g Fiber: 4.6 g Sugar: 0 Protein: 5.5

9. Smoked Mushrooms

Servings: 2

Cooking Time: 45 Minutes

Ingredients:

- 4 cups whole baby portobello, cleaned
- 1 tbsp canola oil
- 1 tbsp onion powder
- 1 tbsp garlic, granulated
- 1 tbsp salt
- 1 tbsp pepper

Directions:

1. Place all the ingredients in a bowl, mix, and combine.
2. Set yours to 180F.
3. Place the mushrooms on the grill directly and smoke for about 30 minutes.
4. Increase heat to high and cook the mushroom for another 15 minutes.
5. Serve warm and enjoy!

Nutrition Info: Calories 118, Total fat 7.6g, Saturated fat 0.6g, Total carbs 10.8g, Net carbs 8.3g, Protein 5.4g, Sugars 3.7g, Fiber 2.5g, Sodium 3500mg, Potassium 536mg

10. Cajun Style Grilled Corn

Servings: 4

Cooking Time: 25 Minutes

Ingredients:

- Four ears corn, with husks
- 1tsp dried oregano
- 1tsp paprika
- 1tsp garlic powder
- 1tsp onion powder
- 1/2 tsp kosher salt
- 1/2 tsp ground black pepper
- 1/4 tsp dried thyme
- 1/4 tsp cayenne pepper
- 2tsp butter, melted

Directions:

1. Preheat pellet grill to 375°F.

2. Peel husks back but do not remove. Scrub and remove silks.

3. Mix oregano, paprika, garlic powder, onion powder, salt, pepper, thyme, and cayenne in a small bowl.

4. Brush melted butter over corn.

5. Rub seasoning mixture over each ear of corn. Pull husks up and place corn on grill grates. Grill for about 12-15 minutes, turning occasionally.

6. Remove from grill and allow to cool for about 5 minutes. Remove husks, then serve and enjoy!

Nutrition Info: Calories: 278 Fat: 17.4 g Cholesterol: 40.7 mg Carbohydrate: 30.6 g Fiber: 4.5 g Sugar: 4.6 g Protein: 5.4 g

11. Smoked Baked Beans

Servings: 12

Cooking Time: 3 Hours

Ingredients:

- 1 medium yellow onion diced
- 3 jalapenos
- 56 oz pork and beans
- 3/4 cup barbeque sauce
- 1/2 cup dark brown sugar
- 1/4 cup apple cider vinegar
- 2 tbsp Dijon mustard
- 2 tbsp molasses

Directions:

1. Preheat, the smoker to 250°F. Pour the beans along with all the liquid in a pan. Add brown sugar, barbeque sauce, Dijon mustard, apple cider vinegar, and molasses. Stir. Place the pan on one of the racks. Smoke for 3 hours until thickened. Remove after 3 hours. Serve

Nutrition Info: Calories: 214 Cal Fat: 2 g Carbohydrates: 42 g Protein: 7 g Fiber: 7 g

12. Split Pea Soup With Mushrooms

Servings: 4

Cooking Time: 35 Minutes

Ingredients:

- 2tbsp. Olive Oil
- 3Garlic cloves, minced
- 3tbsp. Parsley, fresh and chopped
- 2Carrots chopped
- 1.2/3 cup Green Peas
- 9cups Water
- 2tsp. Salt
- 1/4 tsp. Black Pepper

- 1lb. Portobello Mushrooms
- 1Bay Leaf
- 2Celery Ribs, chopped
- 1Onion quartered
- 1/2 tsp. Thyme, dried
- 6tbsp. Parmesan Cheese, grated

Directions:

1. First, keep oil, onion, and garlic in the blender pitcher.
2. Next, select the 'saute' button.
3. Once sautéed, stir in the rest of the ingredients, excluding parsley and cheese.
4. Then, press the 'hearty soup' button.
5. Finally, transfer the soup among the serving bowls and garnish it with parsley and cheese.

Nutrition Info: Calories: 61 Fat: 1.1 g Total Carbs: 10 g Fiber: 1.9 g Sugar: 3.2 g Protein: 3.2 g Cholesterol: 0

13. Smoked Brussels Sprouts

Servings: 6

Cooking Time: 45 Minutes

Ingredients:

- 1-1/2 pounds Brussels sprouts
- Two cloves of garlic minced
- 2 tbsp extra virgin olive oil
- Sea salt and cracked black pepper

Directions:

1. Rinse sprouts
2. Remove the outer leaves and brown bottoms off the sprouts.
3. Place sprouts in a large bowl, then coat with olive oil.
4. Add a coat of garlic, salt, and pepper and transfer them to the pan.
5. Add to the top rack of the smoker with water and woodchips.
6. Smoke for 45 minutes or until it reaches 250°F temperature.

7. Serve

Nutrition Info: Calories: 84 Cal Fat: 4.9 g Carbohydrates: 7.2 g Protein: 2.6 g Fiber: 2.9 g

14. Roasted Green Beans With Bacon

Servings: 6

Cooking Time: 20 Minutes

Ingredients:

- 1-pound green beans
- 4 strips bacon, cut into small pieces
- 4 tablespoons extra virgin olive oil
- 2 cloves garlic, minced
- 1 teaspoon salt

Directions:

1. Fire the grill to 400F. Use desired wood pellets when cooking. Close the lid and preheat for 15 minutes.

2. Toss all ingredients on a sheet tray and spread out evenly.

3. Place the tray on the grill grate and roast for 20 minutes.

Nutrition Info: Calories per serving: 65 ; Protein: 1.3g; Carbs: 3.8g; Fat: 5.3g Sugar: 0.6g

15. Stuffed Grilled Zucchini

Servings: 4

Cooking Time: 10 Minutes

Ingredients:

- 4 zucchini, medium
- 5 tbsp olive oil, divided
- 2 tbsp red onion, finely chopped

- 1/4 tbsp garlic, minced
- 1/2 cup bread crumbs, dry
- 1/2 cup shredded mozzarella cheese, part-skim
- 1/2 tbsp salt
- 1 tbsp fresh mint, minced
- 3 tbsp parmesan cheese, grated

Directions:

1. Halve zucchini lengthwise and scoop pulp ou. Leave 1/4 -inch shell. Now brush using 2 tbsp oil, set aside, and chop the pulp.
2. Saute onion and pulp in a skillet, large, then add garlic and cook for about 1 minute.
3. Add bread crumbs and cook while stirring for about 2 minutes until golden brown.
4. Remove everything from heat, then stir in mozzarella cheese, salt, and mint. Scoop into the zucchini shells and splash with parmesan cheese.
5. Preheat yours to 375F.
6. Place stuffed zucchini on the grill and grill while covered for about 8-10 minutes until tender.
7. Serve warm and enjoy.

Nutrition Info: Calories 186, Total fat 10g, Saturated fat 3g, Total carbs 17g, Net carbs 14g, Protein 9g, Sugars 4g, Fiber 3g, Sodium 553mg, Potassium 237mg

16. Grilled Zucchini

Servings: 6

Cooking Time: 10 Minutes

Ingredients:

- 4 medium zucchini
- 2 tablespoons olive oil
- 1 tablespoon sherry vinegar
- 2 sprigs of thyme, leaves chopped
- ½ teaspoon salt
- 1/3 teaspoon ground black pepper

Directions:

1. Switch on the grill, fill the grill hopper with oak flavored wood pellets, power the grill on by using the control panel, select 'smoke' on the temperature dial, or set the temperature to 350 degrees F and let it preheat for a minimum of 5 minutes.

2. Meanwhile, cut the ends of each zucchini, cut each in half, and then into thirds and place in a plastic bag.
3. Add remaining ingredients, seal the bag, and shake well to coat zucchini pieces.
4. When the grill has preheated, open the lid, place zucchini on the grill grate, shut the grill, and smoke for 4 minutes per side.
5. When done, transfer zucchini to a dish, garnish with more thyme and then serve.

Nutrition Info: Calories: 74 Cal ;Fat: 5.4 g ;Carbs: 6.1 g ;Protein: 2.6 g ;Fiber: 2.3 g

Poultry Recipes

17. Wings

Servings: 4

Cooking Time: 15 Minutes

Ingredients:

- Fresh chicken wings
- Salt to taste
- Pepper to taste
- Garlic powder
- Onion powder
- Cayenne
- Paprika
- Seasoning salt
- Barbeque sauce to taste

Directions:

1. Preheat the wood pellet grill to low. Mix seasoning and coat on chicken. Put the wings on the grill and cook. Place the wings on the grill and cook for 20 minutes or until the wings are fully cooked. Let rest cool for 5 minutes, then toss with barbeque sauce. Serve with orzo and salad. Enjoy.

Nutrition Info: Calories: 311 Cal Fat: 22 g Carbohydrates: 22 g Protein: 22 g Fiber: 3 g

18. Grilled Chicken

Servings: 6

Cooking Time: 1 Hour 10 Minutes;

Ingredients:

- 5 lb. whole chicken
- 1/2 cup oil
- chicken rub

Directions:

1. Preheat on the smoke setting with the lid open for 5 minutes. Close the lid and let it heat for 15 minutes or until it reaches 450...

2. Use baker's twine to tie the chicken legs together, then rub it with oil. Coat the chicken with the rub and place it on the grill.

3. Grill for 70 minutes with the lid closed or until it reaches an internal temperature of 165F.

4. Remove the chicken from the and let rest for 15 minutes. Cut and serve.

Nutrition Info: Calories 935, Total fat 53g, Saturated fat 15g, Total carbs 5g, Net carbs 2g Protein 107g, Sugars 0g, Fiber 2g, Sodium 320mg

19. Smoked Turkey Breast

Servings: 2 To 4

Cooking Time: 1 To 2 Hours

Ingredients:

- 1 (3-pound) turkey breast
- Salt

- Freshly ground black pepper
- 1 teaspoon garlic powder

Directions:

1. Supply your smoker with wood pellets and follow the manufacturer's specific start-up procedure. Preheat the grill, with the lid closed, to 180°F.
2. Season the turkey breast all over with salt, pepper, and garlic powder.
3. Place the breast directly on the grill grate and smoke for 1 hour.
4. Increase the grill's temperature to 350°F and continue to cook until the turkey's internal temperature reaches 170°F. Remove the breast from the grill and serve immediately.

20. Mini Turducken Roulade

Servings: 6

Cooking Time: 2 Hours

Ingredients:

- 1 (16-ounce) boneless turkey breast

- 1 (8-to 10-ounce) boneless duck breast
- 1 (8-ounce) boneless, skinless chicken breast
- Salt
- Freshly ground black pepper
- 2 cups Italian dressing
- 2 tablespoons Cajun seasoning
- 1 cup prepared seasoned stuffing mix
- 8 slices bacon
- Butcher's string

Directions:

1. Butterfly the turkey, duck, and chicken breasts, cover with plastic wrap, and, using a mallet, flatten each ½ inch thick.
2. Season all the meat on both sides with a little salt and pepper.
3. In a medium bowl, combine the Italian dressing and Cajun seasoning. Spread one-fourth of the mixture on top of the flattened turkey breast.
4. Place the duck breast on top of the turkey, spread it with one-fourth of the dressing mixture, and top with the stuffing mix.
5. Place the chicken breast on top of the duck and spread with one-fourth of the dressing mixture.
6. Supply your smoker with wood pellets and follow the manufacturer's specific start-up procedure. Preheat, with the lid, closed to 275°F.

7. Tightly roll up the stack, tie with butcher's string, and slather the whole thing with the remaining dressing mixture.

8. Wrap the bacon slices around the turducken and secure with toothpicks, or try making a bacon weave (see the technique for this in the Jalapeño-Bacon Pork Tenderloin recipe).

9. Place the turducken roulade in a roasting pan. Transfer to the grill, close the lid, and roast for 2 hours, or until a meat thermometer inserted in the turducken reads 165°F. Tent with aluminum foil in the last 30 minutes, if necessary, to keep from over-browning.

10. Let the turducken rest for 15 to 20 minutes before carving. Serve warm.

21. Herb Roasted Turkey

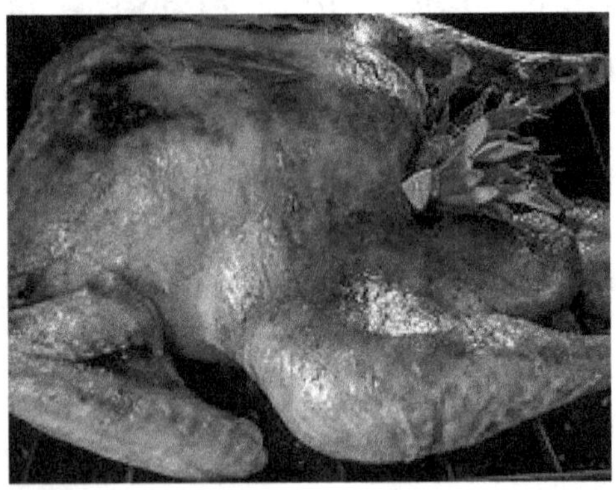

Servings: 12

Cooking Time: 3 Hours And 30 Minutes

Ingredients:

- 14 pounds turkey, cleaned
- Two tablespoons chopped mixed herbs

- Pork and poultry rub as needed
- 1/4 teaspoon ground black pepper
- Three tablespoons butter, unsalted, melted
- Eight tablespoons butter, unsalted, softened
- 2 cups chicken broth

Directions:

1. Clean the turkey by removing the giblets, wash it inside out, pat dry with paper towels, then place it on a roasting pan and tuck the turkey wings by tiring with butcher's string.
2. Switch on the grill, fill the grill hopper with hickory flavored wood pellets, power the grill on by using the control panel, select 'smoke' on the temperature dial, or set the temperature to 325 degrees F and let it preheat for a minimum of 15 minutes.
3. Meanwhile, prepare herb butter, take a small bowl, place the softened butter in it, add black pepper and mixed herbs, and beat until fluffy.
4. Place some of the prepared herb butter underneath the turkey's skin by using a wooden spoon handle and massage the skin to distribute butter evenly.
5. Then rub the exterior of the turkey with melted butter, season with pork and poultry rub, and pour the broth in the roasting pan.
6. When the grill has preheated, open the lid, place the roasting pan containing turkey on the grill grate, shut the grill, and smoke for 3 hours and 30 minutes until the internal temperature reaches 165 degrees F and the top has turned golden brown.

7. When done, transfer turkey to a cutting board, let it rest for 30 minutes, then carve it into slices and serve.

Nutrition Info: Calories: 154.6 Cal ;Fat: 3.1 g ;Carbs: 8.4 g ;Protein: 28.8 g ;Fiber: 0.4 g

22. Lemon Chicken Breast

Servings: 4

Cooking Time: 30 Minutes

Ingredients:

- 6 chicken breasts, skinless and boneless
- ½ cup oil
- 1-3 fresh thyme sprigs
- 1teaspoon ground black pepper
- 2teaspoon salt
- 2teaspoons honey

- 1garlic clove, chopped
- 1lemon, juiced and zested
- Lemon wedges

Directions:

1. Take a bowl and prepare the marinade by mixing thyme, pepper, salt, honey, garlic, lemon zest, and juice. Mix well until dissolved
2. Add oil and whisk
3. Clean breasts and pat them dry, place in a bag alongside marinade, and let them sit in the fridge for 4 hours
4. Preheat your smoker to 400 degrees F
5. Drain chicken and smoke until the internal temperature reaches 165 degrees, for about 15 minutes
6. Serve and enjoy!

Nutrition Info: Calories: 230 Fats: 7g Carbs: 1g Fiber: 2g

23. Applewood-smoked Whole Turkey

Servings: 6 To 8

Cooking Time: 5 To 6 Hours

Ingredients:

- 1 (10- to 12-pound) turkey, giblets removed
- Extra-virgin olive oil, for rubbing
- ¼ cup poultry seasoning
- 8 tablespoons (1 stick) unsalted butter, melted
- ½ cup apple juice
- 2 teaspoons dried sage
- 2 teaspoons dried thyme

Directions:

1. Supply your smoker with wood pellets and follow the manufacturer's specific start-up procedure. Preheat, with the lid, closed to 250°F.
2. Rub the turkey with oil and season with the poultry seasoning inside and out, getting under the skin.

3. In a bowl, combine the melted butter, apple juice, sage, and thyme to basting.

4. Put the turkey in a roasting pan, place on the grill, close the lid, and grill for 5 to 6 hours, basting every hour until the skin is brown and crispy, or until a meat thermometer inserted in the thickest part of the thigh reads 165°F.

5. Let the bird rest for 15 to 20 minutes before carving.

24. Spatchcocked Turkey

Servings: 10 To 14

Cooking Time: 2 Hours

Ingredients:

- 1 whole turkey
- 2 tablespoons olive oil
- 1 batch Chicken Rub

Directions:

1. Supply your smoker with wood pellets and follow the manufacturer's specific start-up procedure. Preheat the grill, with the lid closed, to 350°F.
2. To remove the turkey's backbone, place the turkey on a work surface, on its breast. Using kitchen shears, cut along one side of the turkey's backbone and then the other. Pull out the bone.
3. Once the backbone is removed, turn the turkey breast-side up and flatten it.
4. Coat the turkey with olive oil and season it on both sides with the rub. Using your hands, work the rub into the meat and skin.
5. Place the turkey directly on the grill grate, breast-side up, and cook until its internal temperature reaches 170°F.
6. Remove the turkey from the grill and let it rest for 10 minutes before carving and serving.

25. Garlic Parmesan Chicken Wings

Servings: 6

Cooking Time: 20 Minutes

Ingredients:

- 5 pounds of chicken wings
- 1/2 cup chicken rub
- 3 tablespoons chopped parsley
- 1 cup shredded parmesan cheese
- For the Sauce:
- 5 teaspoons minced garlic
- 2 tablespoons chicken rub
- 1 cup butter, unsalted

Directions:

1. Switch on the grill, fill the grill hopper with cherry flavored wood pellets, power the grill on by using the control panel, select 'smoke' on the temperature dial, or set the temperature to 450 degrees F and let it preheat for a minimum of 15 minutes.

2. Meanwhile, take a large bowl, place chicken wings in it, sprinkle with chicken rub, and toss until well coated.

3. When the grill has preheated, open the lid, place chicken wings on the grill grate, shut the grill, and smoke for 10 minutes per side until the internal temperature reaches 165 degrees F.

4. Meanwhile, prepare the sauce and for this, take a medium saucepan, place it over medium heat, add all the ingredients for the sauce in it and cook for 10 minutes until smooth, set aside until required.

5. When done, transfer chicken wings to a dish, top with prepared sauce, toss until mixed, garnish with cheese and parsley and then serve.

Nutrition Info: Calories: 180 Cal ;Fat: 1 g ;Carbs: 8 g ;Protein: 0 g ;Fiber: 0 g

26. Trager Smoked Spatchcock Turkey

Servings: 8

Cooking Time: 1 Hour 15 Minutes;

Ingredients:

- 1 turkey
- 1/2 cup melted butter
- 1/4 cup chicken rub
- 1 tbsp onion powder
- 1 tbsp garlic powder
- 1 tbsp rubbed sage

Directions:

1. Preheat your to high temperature.
2. Place the turkey on a chopping board with the breast side down and the legs pointing towards you.
3. Cut either side of the turkey backbone to remove the spine. Flip the turkey and place it on a pan
4. Season both sides with the seasonings and place it on the grill skin side up on the grill.
5. Cook for 30 minutes, reduce temperature, and cook for 45 more minutes or until the internal temperature reaches 165F.
6. Remove from the and let rest for 15 minutes before slicing and serving.

Nutrition Info: Calories 156, Total fat 16g, Saturated fat 2g, Total carbs 1g, Net carbs 1g Protein 2g, Sugars 2g, Fiber 5g, Sodium 19mg

27. Grilled Buffalo Chicken Legs

Servings: 8

Cooking Time: 1 Hour 15 Minutes;

Ingredients:

- 12 chicken legs
- 1/2 tbsp salt
- 1 tbsp buffalo seasoning
- 1 cup Buffalo sauce

Directions:

1. Preheat your to 325F.
2. Toss the chicken legs in salt and seasoning, then place them on the preheated grill.
3. Grill for 40 minutes, turning twice through the cooking.
4. Increase the heat and cook for ten more minutes. Brush the chicken legs and brush with buffalo sauce. Cook for an additional 10 minutes or until the internal temperature reaches 165F.
5. Remove from the and brush with more buffalo sauce.
6. Serve with blue cheese, celery, and hot ranch.

Nutrition Info: Calories 956, Total fat 47g, Saturated fat 13g, Total carbs 1g, Net carbs 1g Protein 124g, Sugars 0g, Fiber 0g, Sodium 1750mg

Beef, Pork & Lamb Recipes

28. County Ribs

Preparation Time: 15 Minutes

Cooking Time: 3 Hours

Servings: 4

Ingredients:

- 4 pounds country-style ribs
- Pork ribs to taste.
- 2 cups apple juice
- ½ stick butter, melted.
- 18 ounces BBQ sauce

Directions:

1. Take your drip pan and add water. Cover with aluminum foil.
2. Pre-heat your smoker to 275 degrees F
3. Season country style ribs from all sides
4. Use water fill water pan halfway through and place it over drip pan.
5. Add wood chips to the side tray.
6. Transfer the ribs to your smoker and smoke for 1 hour and 15 minutes until the internal temperature reaches 160 degrees F.
7. Take foil pan and mix melted butter, apple juice, 15 ounces BBQ sauce and put ribs back in the pan, cover with foil.
8. Transfer back to smoker and smoke for 1 hour 15 minutes more until the internal temperature reaches 195 degrees F.
9. Take ribs out from liquid, place them on racks, glaze ribs with more BBQ sauce, and smoke for 10 minutes more.
10. Take them out and let them rest for 10 minutes, serve, and enjoy!

Nutrition:

Calories: 251

Fat: 25g

Carbohydrates: 35g

Protein: 76g

29. Wow-Pork Tenderloin

Preparation Time: 15 Minutes

Cooking Time: 3 Hours

Servings: 4

Ingredients:

- One pork tenderloin
- ¼ cup BBQ sauce
- Three tablespoons dry rub

Directions:

1. Take your drip pan and add water. Cover with aluminum foil.
2. Pre-heat your smoker to 225 degrees F
3. Rub the spice blend all finished the pork tenderloin.
4. Use water fill water pan halfway through and place it over drip pan.

5. Add wood chips to the side tray.
6. Transfer pork meat to your smoker and smoke for 3 hours until the internal temperature reaches 145 degrees F.
7. Brush the BBQ sauce over pork and let it rest.
8. Serve and enjoy!

Nutrition:

Calories: 405

Fat: 9g

Carbohydrates: 15g

Protein: 59g

30. Awesome Pork Shoulder

Preparation Time: 15 Minutes + 24 Hours

Cooking Time: 12 Hours

Servings: 4

Ingredients:

- 8 pounds of pork shoulder

For Rub

- One teaspoon dry mustard
- One teaspoon black pepper
- One teaspoon cumin
- One teaspoon oregano
- One teaspoon cayenne pepper
- 1/3 cup salt
- ¼ cup garlic powder

- ½ cup paprika
- 1/3 cup brown sugar
- 2/3 cup sugar

Directions:

1. Bring your pork under salted water for 18 hours.
2. Pull the pork out from the brine and let it sit for 1 hour.
3. Rub mustard all over the pork.
4. Take a bowl and mix all rub ingredients. Rub mixture all over the meat.
5. Wrap meat and leave it overnight.
6. Take your drip pan and add water. Cover with aluminum foil. Pre-heat your smoker to 250 degrees F
7. Use water fill water pan halfway through and place it over drip pan. Add wood chips to the side tray.
8. Transfer meat to smoker and smoke for 6 hours
9. Take the pork out and wrap in foil, smoke for 6 hours more at 195 degrees F.
10. Shred and serve.
11. Enjoy!

Nutrition:

Calories: 965

Fat: 65g

Carbohydrates: 19g

Protein: 71g

31. Premium Sausage Hash

Preparation Time: 30 Minutes

Cooking Time: 45 Minutes

Servings: 4

Ingredients:

- Nonstick cooking spray
- Two finely minced garlic cloves

- One teaspoon basil, dried
- One teaspoon oregano, dried
- One teaspoon onion powder
- One teaspoon of salt
- 4-6 cooked smoker Italian Sausage (Sliced)
- One large-sized bell pepper, diced.
- One large onion, diced.
- Three potatoes cut into 1-inch cubes.
- Three tablespoons of olive oil
- French bread for serving.

Directions:

1. Pre-heat your smoker to 225 degrees Fahrenheit using your desired wood chips.
2. Cover the smoker grill rack with foil and coat with cooking spray.
3. Take a small bowl and add garlic, oregano, basil, onion powder, and season the mix with salt and pepper.
4. Take a large bowl and add sausage slices, bell pepper, potatoes, onion, olive oil, and spice mix.
5. Mix well and spread the mixture on your foil-covered rack.
6. Place the rack in your smoker and smoke for 45 minutes.

7. Serve with your French bread.
8. Enjoy!

Nutrition:

Calories: 193

Fats: 10g

Carbs: 15g

Fiber: 2g

32. Explosive Smoky Bacon

Preparation Time: 20 Minutes

Cooking Time: 2 Hours and 10 Minutes

Servings: 10

Ingredients:

- 1-pound thick-cut bacon
- One tablespoon BBQ spice rub
- 2 pounds bulk pork sausage
- One cup cheddar cheese, shredded.
- Four garlic cloves, minced.
- 18 ounces BBQ sauce

Directions:

1. Take your drip pan and add water. Cover with aluminum foil.
2. Pre-heat your smoker to 225 degrees F
3. Use water fill water pan halfway through and place it over drip pan.
4. Add wood chips to the side tray.
5. Reserve about ½ a pound of your bacon for cooking later
6. Lay 2 strips of your remaining bacon on a clean surface in an X formation.
7. Alternate the horizontal and vertical bacon strips by waving them tightly in an over and under to create a lattice-like pattern.
8. Sprinkle one teaspoon of BBQ rub over the woven bacon
9. Arrange ½ a pound of your bacon in a large-sized skillet and cook them for 10 minutes over medium-high heat.
10. Drain the cooked slices on a kitchen towel and crumble them.

11. Place your sausages in a large-sized re-sealable bag.
12. While the sausages are still in the bag, roll them out to a square with the same size as the woven bacon.
13. Cut off the bag from the sausage and arrange the sausage over the woven bacon.
14. Toss away the bag.
15. Sprinkle some crumbled bacon, green onions, cheddar cheese, and garlic over the rolled sausages.
16. Pour about ¾ bottle of your BBQ sauce over the sausage and season with some more BBQ rub.
17. Roll up the woven bacon tightly all around the sausage, forming a loaf.
18. Cook the bacon-sausage loaf in your smoker for about one and a ½ hours.
19. Brush up the woven bacon with the remaining BBQ sauce and keep smoking for about 30 minutes until the center of the loaf is no longer pink.
20. Use an instant thermometer to check if the internal temperature is at least 165 degrees Fahrenheit.
21. If yes, then take it out and let it rest for 30 minutes.
22. Slice and serve!

Nutrition:

Calories: 507

Fats: 36g

Carbs: 20g

Fiber: 2g

33. Grilled Lamb Burgers

Preparation Time: 10 minutes

Cooking Time: 15 minutes

Servings: 5

Ingredients:

- 1 1/4 pounds of ground lamb.
- One egg.
- One teaspoon of dried oregano.
- One teaspoon of dry sherry.
- One teaspoon of white wine vinegar.
- Four minced cloves of garlic.

- Red pepper
- 1/2 cup of chopped green onions.
- One tablespoon of chopped mint.
- Two tablespoons of chopped cilantro.
- Two tablespoons of dry breadcrumbs.
- 1/8 teaspoon of salt to taste.
- 1/4 teaspoon of ground black pepper to taste.
- Five hamburger buns.

Directions:

1. Preheat a Wood Pellet Smoker or Grill to 350-450 degrees F, then grease it grates.
2. Using a large mixing bowl, add all the ingredients on the list aside from the buns, then mix properly to combine with clean hands.
3. Make about five patties out of the mixture, then set aside.
4. Place the lamb patties on the preheated grill and cook for about seven to nine minutes, turning only once until an inserted thermometer reads 160 degrees F.
5. Serve the lamb burgers on the hamburger, add your favorite toppings, and enjoy.

Nutrition:

Calories: 376 Cal

Fat: 18.5 g

Carbohydrates: 25.4 g

Protein: 25.5 g

Fiber: 1.6 g

34. Lamb Chops

Preparation Time: 10 minutes

Cooking Time: 12 minutes

Servings: 6

Ingredients:

- 6 (6-ounce) lamb chops
- 3 tablespoons olive oil

- Ground black pepper

Directions:

1. Preheat the pallet grill to 450 degrees F.
2. Coat the lamb chops with oil and then season with salt and black pepper evenly.
3. Arrange the chops in a pallet grill grate and cook for about 4-6 minutes per side.

Nutrition:

Calories: 376 Cal

Fat: 19.5 g

Carbohydrates: 0 g

Protein: 47.8 g

Fiber: 0 g

35. Lamb Ribs Rack

Preparation Time: 10 minutes

Cooking Time: 2 hours

Servings: 2

Ingredients:

- Two tablespoons fresh sage
- Two tablespoons fresh rosemary
- Two tablespoons fresh thyme
- Two peeled garlic cloves
- One tablespoon honey
- Black pepper
- ¼ cup olive oil
- 1 (1½-pound) trimmed rack lamb ribs.

Directions:

1. Combine all ingredients.
2. While the motor is running, slowly add oil and pulse till a smooth paste is formed.
3. Coat the rib rack with paste generously and refrigerate for about 2 hours.
4. Preheat the pallet grill to 225 degrees F.
5. Arrange the rib rack in pallet grill and cook for about 2 hours.
6. Remove the rib rack from the pallet grill and transfer onto a cutting board for about 10-15 minutes before slicing.
7. With a sharp knife, cut the rib rack into equal-sized individual ribs and serve.

Nutrition:

Calories: 826 Cal

Fat: 44.1 g

Carbohydrates: 5.4 g

Protein: 96.3 g

Fiber: 1 g

36. Leg of a Lamb

Preparation Time: 10 minutes

Cooking Time: 2 hours and 30 minutes

Servings: 10

Ingredients:

- 1 (8-ounce) package softened cream cheese.
- ¼ cup cooked and crumbled bacon.
- One seeded and chopped jalapeño pepper.
- One tablespoon crushed dried rosemary.
- Two teaspoons garlic powder
- One teaspoon onion powder
- One teaspoon paprika
- One teaspoon cayenne pepper

- Salt, to taste
- 1 (4-5-pound) butterflied leg of lamb
- 2-3 tablespoons olive oil

Directions:

1. For filling in a bowl, add all ingredients and mix till well combined.
2. For spice mixture in another small bowl, mix all ingredients.
3. Place the leg of lamb onto a smooth surface. Sprinkle the inside of the leg with some spice mixture.
4. Place filling mixture over the inside surface evenly. Roll the leg of lamb tightly, and with a butcher's twine, tie the roll to secure the filling.
5. Coat the outer side of the roll with olive oil evenly, and then sprinkle with spice mixture.
6. Preheat the pallet grill to 225-240 degrees F.
7. Arrange the leg of lamb in a pallet grill and cook for about 2-2½ hours. Remove the leg of lamb from the pallet grill and transfer it onto a cutting board.
8. With a piece of foil, cover the leg loosely and transfer onto a cutting board for about 20-25 minutes before slicing.
9. With a sharp knife, cut the leg of lamb in desired sized slices and serve.

Nutrition:

Calories: 715 Cal

Fat: 38.9 g

Carbohydrates: 2.2 g

Protein: 84.6 g

Fiber: 0.1 g

37. Lamb Breast

Preparation Time: 10 minutes

Cooking Time: 2 hours and 40 minutes

Servings: 2

Ingredients:

- 1 (2-pound) trimmed bone-in lamb breast.
- ½ cup white vinegar

- ¼ cup yellow mustard
- ½ cup BBQ rub

Directions:

1. Preheat the pallet grill to 225 degrees F.
2. Rinse the lamb breast with vinegar evenly.
3. Coat lamb breast with mustard and season with BBQ rub evenly.
4. Arrange lamb breast in pallet grill and cook for about 2-2½ hours.
5. Remove the lamb breast from the pallet grill and transfer onto a cutting board for about 10 minutes before slicing.
6. With a sharp knife, cut the lamb breast in desired-sized slices and serve.

Nutrition:

Calories: 877 Cal

Fat: 34.5 g

Carbohydrates: 2.2 g

Protein: 128.7 g

Fiber: 0 g

38. New York Strip

Servings: 6

Cooking Time: 15 Minutes

Ingredients:

- 3 New York strips
- Salt and pepper

Directions:

1. If the steak is in the fridge, remove it 30 minutes before cooking.
2. Preheat the
3. to 450F.
4. Meanwhile, season the steak generously with salt and pepper. Place it on the grill and let it cook for 5 minutes per side or until the internal temperature reaches 1280F.
5. Rest for 10 minutes.

Nutrition Info: Calories: 198 Cal Fat: 14 g Carbohydrates: 0 g Protein: 17 g Fiber: 0 g

39. Lamb Shank

Servings: 6

Cooking Time: 4 Hours

Ingredients:

- 8-ounce red wine
- 2-ounce whiskey
- 2 tablespoons minced fresh rosemary
- 1 tablespoon minced garlic
- Black pepper
- 6 ($1\frac{1}{4}$-pound) lamb shanks

Directions:

1. In a bowl, add all ingredients except lamb shank and mix till well combined.

2. In a large resealable bag, add marinade and lamb shank.
3. Seal the bag and shake to coat completely.
4. Refrigerate for about 24 hours.
5. Preheat the pallet grill to 225 degrees F.
6. Arrange the leg of lamb in a pallet grill and cook for about 4 hours.

Nutrition Info: Calories: 1507 Cal Fat: 62 g Carbohydrates: 68.7 g Protein:163.3 g Fiber: 6 g

40. Spicy Pork Chops

Servings: 4

Cooking Time: 10-15 Minutes

Ingredients:

- 1 tbsp. olive oil
- 2 cloves garlic, crushed and minced

- 1 tbsp. cayenne pepper
- ½ tsp. hot sauce
- ¼ cup lime juice
- 2 tsp. ground cumin
- 1 tsp. ground cinnamon
- 4 pork chops
- Lettuce

Directions:

1. Mix the olive oil, garlic, cayenne pepper, hot sauce, lime juice, cumin, and cinnamon.
2. Pour the mixture into a re-sealable plastic bag. Place the pork chops inside. Seal and turn to coat evenly. Chill in the refrigerator for 4 hours. Grill for 10 to 15 minutes, flipping occasionally.

Nutrition Info: Calories: 196 Cal Fat: 9 g Carbohydrates: 3 g Protein: 25 g Fiber: 1 g

41. Apple-smoked Bacon

Servings: 4 To 6

Cooking Time: 20 To 30 Minutes

Ingredients:

- 1 (1-pound) package thick-sliced bacon

Directions:

1. Supply your smoker with wood pellets and follow the manufacturer's specific start-up procedure. Preheat the grill, with the lid closed, to 275°F.
2. Supply your smoker with wood pellets and follow the manufacturer's specific start-up procedure. Preheat the grill, with the lid closed, to 275°F.

42. Deliciously Spicy Rack Of Lamb

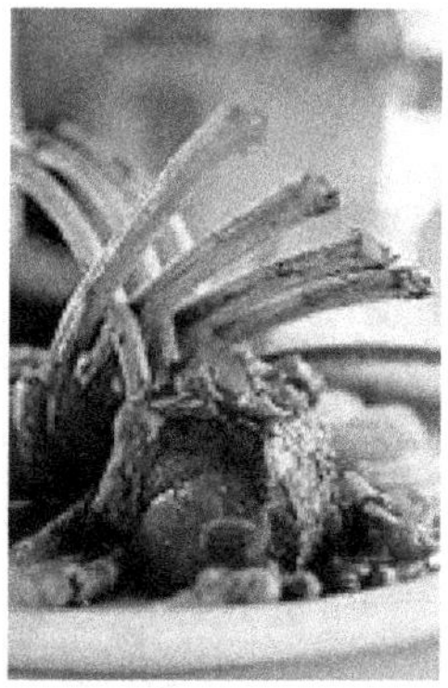

Servings: 6

Cooking Time: 3 Hours

Ingredients:

- 2 tbsp. paprika
- ½ tbsp. coriander seeds
- 1 tsp. cumin seeds
- 1 tsp. ground allspice
- 1 tsp. lemon peel powder
- Salt and freshly ground black pepper, to taste
- 2 (1½-lb.) rack of lamb ribs, trimmed

Directions:

1. Set the Grill temperature to 225 degrees F and preheat with a closed lid for 15 minutes.
2. In a coffee grinder, add all ingredients except rib racks and grind them into a powder.

3. Coat the rib racks with spice mixture generously.
4. Arrange the rib racks onto the grill and cook for about 3 hours.
5. Remove the rib racks from the grill and place them onto a cutting board for about 10-15 minutes before slicing.
6. With a sharp knife, cut the rib racks into equal-sized individual ribs and serve.

Nutrition Info: Calories per serving: 545; Carbohydrates: 1.7g; Protein: 64.4g; Fat: 29.7g; Sugar: 0.3g; Sodium: 221mg; Fiber: 1g

43. Grilled Butter Basted Rib-eye

Servings: 4

Cooking Time: 20 Minutes

Ingredients:

- 2 rib-eye steaks, bone-in
- Slat to taste

- Pepper to taste
- 4 tbsp butter, unsalted

Directions:

1. Mix steak, salt, and pepper in a ziplock bag. Seal the bag and mix until the beef is well coated. Ensure you get as much air as possible from the ziplock bag.
2. Set the wood pellet grill temperature to high with a closed lid for 15 minutes. Place a cast iron into the grill.
3. Place the steaks on the hottest spot of the grill and cook for 5 minutes with the lid closed.
4. Open the lid and add butter to the skillet when it's almost melted. Place the steak on the skillet with the grilled side up.
5. Cook for 5 minutes while busting the meat with butter. Close the lid and cook until the internal temperature is 130°F.
6. Remove the steak from the skillet and let rest for 10 minutes before enjoying with the reserved butter.

Nutrition Info: Calories 745, Total fat 65g, Saturated fat 32g, Total Carbs 5g, Net Carbs 5g, Protein 35g, Sugar 0g, Fiber 0g

44. Pork Belly Burnt Ends

Servings: 8 To 10

Cooking Time: 6 Hours

Ingredients:

- 1 (3-pound) skinless pork belly (if not already skinned, use a sharp boning knife to remove the skin from the belly), cut into 1½- to 2-inch cubes
- One batch Sweet Brown Sugar Rub
- ½ cup honey
- 1 cup The Ultimate BBQ Sauce
- Two tablespoons light brown sugar

Directions:

1. Supply your smoker with wood pellets and follow the manufacturer's specific start-up procedure. Preheat the grill, with the lid closed, to 250°F.
2. Generously season the pork belly cubes with the rub. Using your hands, work the rub into the meat.

3. Place the pork cubes directly on the grill grate and smoke until their internal temperature reaches 195°F.

4. Transfer the cubes from the grill to an aluminum pan. Add the honey, barbecue sauce, and brown sugar. Stir to combine and coat the pork.

5. Place the pan in the grill and smoke the pork for 1 hour, uncovered. Remove the pork from the grill and serve immediately.

45. Simple Grilled Lamb Chops

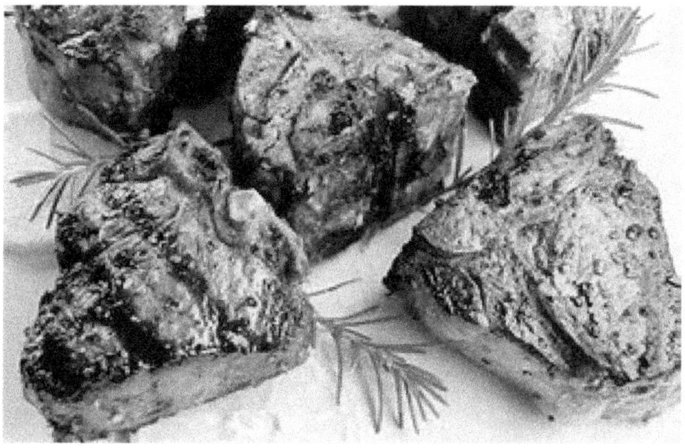

Servings: 6

Cooking Time: 6 Minutes

Ingredients:

- 1/4 cup distilled white vinegar
- 2 tbsp salt
- 1/2 tbsp black pepper

- 1 tbsp garlic, minced
- 1 onion, thinly sliced
- 2 tbsp olive oil
- 2lb lamb chops

Directions:

1. In a resealable bag, mix vinegar, salt, black pepper, garlic, sliced onion, and oil until all salt has dissolved.
2. Add the lamb chops and toss until well coated. Place in the fridge to marinate for 2 hours.
3. Preheat the wood pellet grill to high heat.
4. Remove the lamb from the fridge and discard the marinade. Wrap any exposed bones with foil.
5. Grill the lamb for 3 minutes per side. You can also broil in a broiler for more crispness.
6. Serve and enjoy

Nutrition Info: Calories 519, Total fat 44.8g, Saturated fat 18g, Total Carbs 2.3g, Net Carbs 1.9g, Protein 25g, Sugar1g, Fiber 0.4g, Sodium: 861mg, Potassium 359mg

46. Smoked Sausages

Servings: 4

Cooking Time: 3 Hours

Ingredients:

- 3 pounds ground pork
- 1 tablespoon onion powder
- 1 tablespoon garlic powder
- 1 teaspoon curing salt
- 4 teaspoon black pepper
- 1/2 tablespoon salt
- 1/2 tablespoon ground mustard
- Hog casings, soaked
- 1/2 cup ice water

Directions:

1. Switch on the grill, fill the grill hopper with flavored wood pellets, power the grill on by using the control panel, select 'smoke' on the temperature dial, or set the temperature to 225 degrees F and let it it preheat for a minimum of 15 minutes.

2. Meanwhile, take a medium bowl, place all the ingredients in it except for water and hog casings, and stir until well mixed.

3. Pour in water, stir until incorporated, place the mixture in a sausage stuffer, then stuff the hog casings and tie the link to the desired length.

4. When the grill has preheated, open the lid, place the sausage links on the grill grate, shut the grill, and smoke for 2 to 3 hours until the internal temperature reaches 155 degrees F.

5. When done, transfer sausages to a dish, let them rest for 5 minutes, then slice and serve.

Nutrition Info: Calories: 230 Cal ;Fat: 22 g ;Carbs: 2 g ;Protein: 14 g ;Fiber: 0 g

47. Wood Pellet Smoked Beef Jerky

Servings: 10

Cooking Time: 5 Hours

Ingredients:

- 3 lb sirloin steaks, sliced into 1/4 inch thickness
- 2 cups soy sauce
- 1/2 cup brown sugar
- 1 cup pineapple juice
- 2 tbsp sriracha
- 2 tbsp red pepper flake
- 2 tbsp hoisin
- 2 tbsp onion powder
- 2 tbsp rice wine vinegar
- 2 tbsp garlic, minced

Directions:

1. Mix all the ingredients in a ziplock bag. Seal the bag and mix until the beef is well coated. Ensure you get as much air as possible from the ziplock bag.
2. Put the bag in the fridge overnight to let it marinate. Remove the bag from the fridge for 1 hour prior to cooking.
3. Startup your wood pallet grill and set it to a smoke setting. Layout the meat on the grill with half-inch space between them.
4. Let them cook for 5 hours while turning after every 2-1/2 hours.
5. Transfer from the grill and let cool for 30 minutes before serving.

6. Enjoy.

Nutrition Info: Calories 80, Total fat 1g, Saturated fat 0g, Total carbs 5g, Net carbs 5g, Protein 14g, Sugar 5g, Fiber 0g, Sodium: 650mg

48. Bbq Brisket

Servings: 8

Cooking Time: 10 Hours

Ingredients:

- 1 beef brisket, about 12 pounds
- Beef rub as needed

Directions:

1. Season beef brisket with beef rub until well coated, place it in a large plastic bag, seal it and let it marinate for a minimum of 12 hours in the refrigerator.
2. When ready to cook, switch on the grill, fill the grill hopper with hickory flavored wood pellets, power the grill on by using the control panel, select 'smoke' on the temperature dial, or set the temperature to 225 degrees F and let it preheat for a minimum of 15 minutes.

3. When the grill has preheated, open the lid, place marinated brisket on the grill grate fat-side down, shut the grill, and smoke for 6 hours until the internal temperature reaches 160 degrees F.

4. Then wrap the brisket in foil, return it to the grill grate and cook for 4 hours until the internal temperature reaches 204 degrees F.

5. When done, transfer brisket to a cutting board, let it rest for 30 minutes, then cut it into slices and serve.

Nutrition Info: Calories: 328 Cal ;Fat: 21 g ;Carbs: 0 g ;Protein: 32 g ;Fiber: - g

49. Bacon Stuffed Smoked Pork Loin

Servings: 4 To 6

Cooking Time: 1 Hour

Ingredients:

- 3 Pound Pork Loin, Butterflied
- As Needed Pork Rub
- 1/4 Cup Walnuts, Chopped

- 1/3 Cup Craisins
- 1 Tablespoon Oregano, fresh
- 1 Tablespoon fresh thyme
- 6 Pieces Asparagus, fresh
- 6 Slices Bacon, sliced
- 1/3 Cup Parmesan cheese, grated
- As Needed Bacon Grease

Directions:

1. Lay down two large pieces of butcher's twine on your work surface. Place butterflied pork loin perpendicular to twine.
2. Season the inside of the pork loin with the pork rub.
3. On one end of the loin, layer in a line all of the ingredients, beginning with the chopped walnuts, craisins, oregano, thyme, and asparagus.
4. Add bacon and top with the parmesan cheese.
5. Starting at the end with all of the fillings, carefully roll up the pork loin and secure on both ends with butcher's twine.
6. Roll the pork loin in the reserved bacon grease and season the outside with more Pork Rub.
7. When ready to cook, set temperature to 180°F and preheat, lid closed for 15 minutes. Place stuffed pork loin directly on the grill grate and smoke for 1 hour.
8. Remove the pork loin; increase the temperature to 350°F and allow to preheat.

9. Place the loin back on the and grill for approximately 30 to 45 minutes or until the temperature reads 135°F on an instant-read thermometer.

10. Move the pork loin to a plate and tent it with aluminum foil. Let it rest for 15 minutes before slicing and serving. Enjoy!

50. Smoked Beef Ribs

Preparation Time: 25 minutes

Cooking Time: 4 to 6 hours

Servings: 4 to 8

Ingredients:

- 2 (2- or 3-pound) racks beef ribs
- Two tablespoons yellow mustard
- One batch Sweet and Spicy Cinnamon Rub

Directions:

1. Supply your smoker with wood pellets and follow the manufacturer's specific start-up procedure. Allow your griller to preheat with the lid closed to 225°F.

2. Take off the membrane from the backside of the ribs. This can be done by cutting just through the membrane in an X pattern and working a paper towel between the membrane and the ribs to pull it off.

3. Coat the ribs all over with mustard and season them with the rub. Using your two hands, work with the rub into the meat.

4. Put your ribs directly on the grill grate and smoke until their internal temperature reaches between 190°F and 200°F.

5. Remove the racks from the grill and cut them into individual ribs. Serve immediately.

Nutrition: Calories: 230 Carbs: 0g Fat: 17g Protein: 20g

51. Herbed Beef Eye Fillet

Preparation Time: 15 minutes

Cooking Time: 8 hours

Servings: 6

Ingredients:

- Pepper
- Salt
- Two tablespoons chopped rosemary
- Two tablespoons chopped basil
- Two tablespoons olive oil
- Three cloves crushed garlic
- ¼ cup chopped oregano
- ¼ cup chopped parsley
- 2 pounds beef eye fillet

Directions:

1. Use salt and pepper to rub in the meat before placing it in a container.
2. Place the garlic, oil, rosemary, oregano, basil, and parsley in a bowl. Stir well to combine.
3. Rub the fillet generously with this mixture on all sides. Let the meat sit on the counter for 30 minutes.

4. Add wood pellets to your smoker and follow your cooker's startup procedure. Preheat your smoker, with your lid closed, until it reaches 450.

5. Lay the meat on the grill, cover, and smoke for ten minutes per side or your preferred tenderness.

6. Once it is done to your likeness, allow it to rest for ten minutes. Slice and enjoy.

Nutrition: Calories: 202 Carbs: 0g Fat: 8g Protein: 33g

52. Beer Honey Steaks

Preparation Time: 10 minutes

Cooking Time: 55 minutes

Servings: 4

Ingredients:

- Pepper
- Juice of one lemon

- 1 cup beer of choice
- One tablespoon honey
- Salt
- Two tablespoons olive oil
- One teaspoon thyme
- Four steaks of choice

Directions:

1. Season the steaks with pepper and salt.
2. Combine the olive oil, lemon juice, honey, thyme, and beer.
3. Rub the steaks with this mixture generously.
4. Add wood pellets to your smoker and follow your cooker's startup procedure. Preheat your smoker, with your lid closed, until it reaches 450.
5. Place the steaks onto the grill, cover, and smoke for ten minutes per side.
6. For about 10 minutes, let it cool after removing it from the grill.

Nutrition: Calories: 245 Carbs: 8gFat: 5g Protein: 40g

Fish Seafood Recipes

53. Sweet Honey Soy Smoked Salmon

Preparation time: 15 minutes

Cooking time: 2 hours and 10 minutes

Servings: 10

Ingredients:

- Salmon fillet (4-lbs., 1.8-kg.)

The Brine:

- ¾ cup Brown sugar
- 3 tbsp. Soy sauce
- 3 tsp. Kosher salt
- 3 cups Coldwater

The Glaze:

- 2 tbsp. Butter
- 2 tbsp. Brown sugar

- 2 tbsp. Olive oil
- 2 tbsp. Honey
- 1 tbsp. Soy sauce

The Heat:

- Alder wood pellets

Directions:

1. Add brown sugar, soy sauce, and kosher salt to the cold water, then stir until dissolved.
2. Put the salmon fillet into the brine mixture and soak it for at least 2 hours.
3. After 2 hours, take the salmon fillet out of the brine, then wash and rinse it.
4. Plug the wood pellet smoker and place the wood pellet inside the hopper. Turn the switch on.
5. Set the temperature to 225°F (107°C) and prepare the wood pellet smoker for indirect heat. Wait until the wood pellet smoker is ready.
6. Place the salmon fillet in the wood pellet smoker and smoke it for 2 hours.
7. In the meantime, melt the butter over low heat, then mix it with brown sugar, olive oil, honey, and soy sauce. Mix well.
8. After an hour of smoking, baste the glaze mixture over the salmon fillet and repeat it once every 10 minutes.
9. Smoke until the salmon is flaky and remove it from the wood pellet smoker.

10. Transfer the smoked salmon fillet to a serving dish and baste the remaining glaze mixture over it.

11. Serve and enjoy.

Nutrition:

- Amount per 199 g
- = 1 serving(s)
- Energy (calories): 345 kcal
- Protein: 37.42 g
- Fat: 15.6 g
- Carbohydrates: 11.52 g

54. Cranberry Lemon Smoked Mackerel

Preparation time: 15 minutes

Cooking time: 2 hours and 10 minutes

Servings: 10

Ingredients:

- Mackerel fillet (3.5-lb., 2.3-kg.)

The Brine:

- Three cans of cranberry juice
- ½ cup pineapple juice
- 3 cups cold water
- ¼ cup brown sugar
- Two cinnamon stick
- Two fresh lemons
- Two bay leaves
- Three fresh thyme leaves

The Rub:

- ¾ tsp. kosher salt
- ¾ tsp. pepper

The Heat:

- Alder wood pellets

Directions:

1. Mix the cranberry juice and pineapple juice with water, then stir well.
2. Stir in brown sugar to the liquid mixture, then mix until dissolved.
3. Cut the lemons into slices, then add them to the liquid mixture and cinnamon sticks, bay leaves, and fresh thyme leaves.

4. Put the mackerel fillet into the brine and soak it for at least 2 hours. Store it in the refrigerator to keep the mackerel fillet fresh.
5. After 2 hours, remove the mackerel fillet from the refrigerator and take it out of the brine mixture.
6. Plug the wood pellet smoker and place the wood pellet inside the hopper. Turn the switch on.
7. Set the temperature to 225°F (107°C) and prepare the wood pellet smoker for indirect heat. Wait until the wood pellet smoker is ready.
8. Sprinkle salt and pepper over the mackerel fillet, then place it in the wood pellet smoker.
9. Smoke the mackerel fillet for 2 hours or until it flakes and removes it from the wood pellet smoker.
10. Transfer the smoked mackerel fillet to a serving dish and serve.
11. Enjoy!

Nutrition:

- Amount per 225 g
- = 1 serving(s)
- Energy (calories): 386 kcal
- Protein: 46.11 g
- Fat: 4.56 g
- Carbohydrates: 37.85 g

55. Citrusy Smoked Tuna Belly with Sesame Aro

Preparation time: 15 minutes

Cooking time: 2 hours and 10 minutes

Servings: 10

Ingredients:

- Tuna belly (4-lbs., 1.8-kg.)

The Marinade:

- 3 tbsp. sesame oil
- ½ cup of soy sauce
- 2 tbsp. lemon juice
- ½ cup of orange juice
- 2 tbsp. Chopped fresh parsley
- ½ tsp. oregano

- 1 tbsp. minced garlic
- 2 tbsp. brown sugar
- 1 tsp. Kosher salt
- ½ tsp. pepper

The Glaze:

- 2 tbsp. maple syrup
- 1 tbsp. balsamic vinegar

The Heat:

- Mesquite wood pellets

Directions:

1. Combine sesame oil with soy sauce, lemon juice, and orange juice, then mix well.
2. Add oregano, minced garlic, brown sugar, kosher salt, pepper, chopped parsley to the wet mixture, and then stir until incorporated.
3. Carefully apply the wet mixture over the tuna fillet and marinate it for 2 hours. Store it in the refrigerator to keep the tuna fresh.
4. After 2 hours, remove the marinated tuna from the wood pellet smoker and thaw it at room temperature.
5. Plug the wood pellet smoker and place the wood pellet inside the hopper. Turn the switch on.
6. Set the temperature to 225°F (107°C) and prepare the wood pellet smoker for indirect heat. Wait until the wood pellet smoker is ready.

7. Place the marinated tuna fillet in the wood pellet smoker and smoke it until flaky.
8. Once it is done, remove the smoked tuna fillet from the wood pellet smoker and transfer it to a serving dish.
9. Mix the maple syrup with balsamic vinegar, then baste the mixture over the smoked tuna fillet.
10. Serve and enjoy.

Nutrition:

- Amount per 195 g
- = 1 serving(s)
- Energy (calories): 206 kcal
- Protein: 35.84 g
- Fat: 4.96 g
- Carbohydrates: 4.98 g

56. Savory Smoked Trout with Fennel and Black Pepper Rub

Preparation time: 15 minutes

Cooking time: 2 hours 10 minutes

Servings: 10

Ingredients:

- Trout fillet (4,5-lb., 2.3-kg.)

The Rub:

- 2 tbsp. lemon juice
- 3 tbsp. fennel seeds
- 1 ½ tbsp. ground coriander
- 1 tbsp. Black pepper
- ½ tsp. chili powder

- 1 tsp. kosher salt
- 1 tsp. garlic powder

The Glaze:

- 3 tbsp. olive oil

The Heat:

- Mesquite wood pellets

Directions:

1. Drizzle lemon juice over the trout fillet and let it rest for approximately 10 minutes.
2. In the meantime, combine the fennel seeds with coriander, black pepper, chili powder, salt, and garlic powder, then mix well.
3. Rub the trout fillet with the spice mixture, then set aside.
4. Plug the wood pellet smoker and place the wood pellet inside the hopper. Turn the switch on.
5. Set the temperature to 225°F (107°C) and prepare the wood pellet smoker for indirect heat. Wait until the wood pellet smoker is ready.
6. Place the seasoned trout fillet in the wood pellet smoker and smoke it for 2 hours.
7. Baste olive oil over the trout fillet and repeat it once every 20 minutes.
8. Once the smoked trout flakes, remove it from the wood pellet smoker and transfer it to a serving dish.
9. Serve and enjoy.

Nutrition:

- Energy (calories): 185 kcal
- Protein: 47.32 g
- Fat: 17.18 g
- Carbohydrates: 0.94 g

57. Sweet Smoked Shrimps Garlic Butter

Preparation time: 15 minutes

Cooking time: 20 minutes

Servings: 10

Ingredients:

- Fresh shrimps (2-lbs., 0.9-kg.)

The Rub:

- 2 tbsp. Lemon juice
- ½ tsp. Salt
- ½ tsp. Black pepper

The Glaze:

- 2 tbsp. Butter
- ½ tsp. Garlic powder

The Heat:

- Hickory wood pellets

Directions:

1. Peel the fresh shrimps and drizzle lemon juice over them. Let them rest for several minutes.
2. After that, sprinkle salt and black pepper over the shrimps and spread them in a disposable aluminum pan.
3. Plug the wood pellet smoker and place the wood pellet inside the hopper. Turn the switch on.
4. Set the temperature to 200°F (93°C) and prepare the wood pellet smoker for indirect heat. Wait until the wood pellet smoker is ready.
5. Insert the aluminum pan with shrimps into the wood pellet smoker and smoke the shrimps for approximately 20 minutes.
6. Regularly check the shrimps and once they turn pink, take them out of the wood pellet smoker.

7. Add garlic powder to the butter, then mix until combined. The butter will be soft.

8. Baste the garlic butter over the smoked shrimps and serve.

9. Enjoy!

Nutrition:

- Amount per 94 g
- = 1 serving(s)
- Energy (calories): 99 kcal
- Protein: 18.6 g
- Fat: 2.01 g
- Carbohydrates: 0.21 g

58. Spiced Smoked Crabs with Lemon Grass

Preparation time: 15 minutes

Cooking time: 20 minutes

Servings: 10

Ingredients:

- Fresh crabs (5-lb., 2.3-kg.)

The Rub:

- 2 tbsp. smoked paprika
- 1 tsp. kosher salt
- 2 tbsp. dried parsley
- 2 tbsp. dried thyme
- 1 tbsp. black pepper
- 1 tsp. cayenne pepper

- 1 tsp. Allspice
- ½ tsp. Ground ginger
- ½ tsp. cinnamon powder
- Two lemongrass

The Heat:

- Hickory wood pellets

Directions:

1. Combine the smoked paprika, salt, parsley, thyme, black pepper, ground ginger, cinnamon powder, cayenne pepper, and allspice, then mix well.
2. Arrange the crabs in a disposable aluminum pan, then sprinkle the spice mixture over them.
3. Add lemongrasses on top, then cover the seasoned crabs with aluminum foil.
4. Plug the wood pellet smoker and place the wood pellet inside the hopper. Turn the switch on.
5. Set the temperature to 200°F (93°C) and prepare the wood pellet smoker for indirect heat. Wait until the wood pellet smoker is ready.
6. Insert the aluminum pan with crabs into the wood pellet smoker and smoke the crabs for 30 minutes.
7. Once it is done, take the smoked crabs out of the wood pellet smoker and serve.
8. Enjoy!

Nutrition:

- Amount per 229 g
- = 1 serving(s)
- Energy (calories): 201 kcal
- Protein: 41.14 g
- Fat: 2.58 g
- Carbohydrates: 0.98 g

59. Tequila Orange Marinade Smoked Lobster

Preparation time: 15 minutes

Cooking time: 1 hour 10 minutes

Servings: 10

Ingredients:

- Fresh lobsters (5-lb., 2.3-kg.)

The Marinade:

- ¼ cup Tequila
- 3 tbsp. Lemon juice
- Two cups Orange juice
- ½ tsp. Grated lemon zest
- ½ tsp. Grated orange zest
- 1 tsp. Kosher salt
- ¼ tsp. Pepper

The Heat:

- Hickory wood pellets

Directions:

1. Mix the tequila with lemon juice and orange juice, then stir well.
2. Add grated lemon zest, orange zest, salt, and pepper to the liquid mixture, then stir until dissolved.
3. Drizzle the mixture over the lobsters and marinate them for at least 2 hours. Store the marinated lobsters in the refrigerator to keep them fresh.
4. After 2 hours, take the marinated lobsters out of the refrigerator and thaw them at room temperature.

5. Plug the wood pellet smoker and place the wood pellet inside the hopper. Turn the switch on.
6. Set the temperature to 200°F (93°C) and prepare the wood pellet smoker for indirect heat. Wait until the wood pellet smoker is ready.
7. Arrange the marinated lobsters in the wood pellet smoker and smoke them for an hour or until the smoked lobsters' internal temperature reaches 145°F (63°C).
8. Remove the smoked lobsters from the wood pellet smoker and transfer them to a serving dish.
9. Serve and enjoy.

Nutrition:

- Amount per 192 g
- = 1 serving(s)
- Energy (calories): 189 kcal
- Protein: 37.66 g
- Fat: 1.74 g
- Carbohydrates: 3.42 g

60. Beer Butter Smoked Clams

Preparation time: 15 minutes

Cooking time: 30 minutes

Servings: 10

Ingredients:

- Fresh clams (5-lb., 2.3-kg.)

The Sauce:

- One bottle beer
- 2 tbsp. olive oil
- 2 tbsp. minced garlic
- 1 tsp. salt
- ¼ cup butter

The Heat:

- Hickory wood pellets

Directions:

1. Preheat a saucepan over medium heat, then pour olive oil into it.
2. Once the oil is hot, stir in the minced garlic and sauté until wilted and aromatic.
3. Remove the saucepan from heat, then pour beer into it.
4. Add salt to the mixture, then stir until incorporated.
5. Spread the clams in a disposable aluminum pan, then pour the beer mixture over the clams.
6. Drop butter at several places on top of the clams, then set aside.
7. Plug the wood pellet smoker and place the wood pellet inside the hopper. Turn the switch on.
8. Set the temperature to 200°F (93°C) and prepare the wood pellet smoker for indirect heat. Wait until the wood pellet smoker is ready.
9. Insert the aluminum pan with clams into the wood pellet smoker and smoke the clams for half an hour.
10. Once it is done and the smoked clams' shells are open, take them out of the wood pellet smoker.
11. Transfer the smoked clams to a serving dish and enjoy.

Nutrition:

- Amount per 138 g
- = 1 serving(s)

- Energy (calories): 137 kcal
- Protein: 1.51 g
- Fat: 3.41 g
- Carbohydrates: 25.12 g

61. Bbq Oysters

Servings: 4-6

Cooking Time: 16 Minutes

Ingredients:

- Shucked oysters - 12
- Unsalted butter - 1 lb.
- Chopped green onions - 1 bunch
- Honey Hog BBQ Rub or Meat Church "The Gospel" - 1 tbsp
- Minced green onions - ½ bunch

- Seasoned breadcrumbs - ½ cup
- Cloves of minced garlic - 2
- Shredded pepper jack cheese - 8 oz
- Heat and Sweet BBQ sauce

Directions:

1. Preheat the pellet grill for about 10-15 minutes with the lid closed.
2. To make the compound butter, wait for the butter to soften. Then combine the butter, onions, BBQ rub, and garlic thoroughly.
3. Lay the butter evenly on plastic wrap or parchment paper. Roll it up in a log shape and tie the ends with butcher's twine. Place these in the freezer to solidify for an hour. This butter can be used on any kind of grilled meat to enhance its flavor. Any other high-quality butter can also replace this compound butter.
4. Shuck the oysters, keeping the juice in the shell.
5. Sprinkle all the oysters with breadcrumbs and place them directly on the grill. Allow them to cook for 5 minutes. You will know they are cooked when the oysters begin to curl slightly at the edges.
6. Once they are cooked, put a spoonful of the compound butter on the oysters. Once the butter melts, you can add a little bit of pepper jack cheese to add more flavor to them.
7. The oysters must not be on the grill for longer than 6 minutes, or you risk overcooking them. Put a generous squirt of the BBQ sauce on all the oysters. Also, add a few chopped onions.
8. Allow them to cool for a few minutes and enjoy the taste of the sea!

Nutrition Info: Carbohydrates: 2.5 g Protein: 4.7 g Fat: 1.1 g Sodium: 53 mg Cholesterol: 25 mg

62. Blackened Catfish

Servings: 4

Cooking Time: 40 Minutes

Ingredients:

- Spice blend
- 1teaspoon granulated garlic
- 1/4 teaspoon cayenne pepper
- 1/2 cup Cajun seasoning
- 1teaspoon ground thyme
- 1teaspoon ground oregano
- 1teaspoon onion powder
- 1tablespoon smoked paprika

- 1teaspoon pepper
- Fish
- 4 catfish fillets
- Salt to taste
- 1/2 cup butter

Directions:

1. In a bowl, combine all the ingredients for the spice blend.
2. Sprinkle both sides of the fish with the salt and spice blend.
3. Set your wood pellet grill to 450 degrees F.
4. Heat your cast iron pan and add the butter. Add the fillets to the pan.
5. Cook for 5 minutes per side.
6. Serving Suggestion: Garnish with lemon wedges.
7. Tip: Smoke the catfish for 20 minutes before seasoning.

Nutrition Info: Calories: 181.5 Fat: 10.5 g Cholesterol: 65.8 mg Carbohydrates: 2.9 g Fiber: 1.8 g Sugars: 0.4 g Protein: 19.2 g

63. Grilled Shrimp

Servings: 4

Cooking Time: 15 Minutes

Ingredients:

- Jumbo shrimp peeled and cleaned - 1 lb.
- Oil - 2 tbsp
- Salt - ½ tbsp
- Skewers - 4-5
- Pepper - ⅛ tbsp
- Garlic salt - ½ tbsp

Directions:

1. Preheat the wood pellet grill to 375 degrees.
2. Mix all the ingredients in a small bowl.
3. After washing and drying the shrimp, mix it well with the oil and seasonings.

4. Add skewers to the shrimp and set the bowl of shrimp aside.

5. Open the skewers and flip them.

6. Cook for four more minutes. Remove when the shrimp is opaque and pink.

Nutrition Info: Carbohydrates: 1.3 g Protein: 19 g Fat: 1.4 g Sodium: 805 mg Cholesterol: 179 mg

64. Grilled Lobster Tail

Servings: 4

Cooking Time: 15 Minutes

Ingredients:

- 2 (8 ounces each) lobster tails
- 1/4 tsp old bay seasoning
- ½ tsp oregano
- 1 tsp paprika
- Juice from one lemon

- 1/4 tsp Himalayan salt
- 1/4 tsp freshly ground black pepper
- 1/4 tsp onion powder
- 2 tbsp freshly chopped parsley
- ¼ cup melted butter

Directions:

1. Slice the tail in the middle with a kitchen shear. Pull the shell apart slightly and run your hand through the meat to separate the meat partially
2. Combine the seasonings
3. Drizzle lobster tail with lemon juice and season generously with the seasoning mixture.
4. Preheat your wood pellet smoker to 450°F using applewood pellets.
5. Place the lobster tail directly on the grill grate, meat side down. Cook for about 15 minutes.
6. The tails must be pulled off, and it must cool down for a few minutes
7. Drizzle melted butter over the tails.
8. Serve and garnish with fresh chopped parsley.

Nutrition Info: Calories: 146 Cal Fat: 11.7 g Carbohydrates: 2.1 g Protein: 9.3 g Fiber: 0.8 g

65. Stuffed Shrimp Tilapia

Servings: 5

Cooking Time: 45 Minutes

Ingredients:

- 5 ounces fresh, farmed tilapia fillets
- 2 tablespoons extra virgin olive oil
- 1and ½ teaspoons smoked paprika
- 1and ½ teaspoons Old Bay seasoning
- Shrimp stuffing
- 1pound shrimp, cooked and deveined
- 1tablespoon salted butter
- 1cup red onion, diced
- 1cup Italian bread crumbs
- ½ cup mayonnaise
- 1large egg, beaten

- 2teaspoons fresh parsley, chopped
- 1and ½ teaspoons salt and pepper

Directions:

1. Take a food processor and add shrimp, chop them up
2. Take a skillet and place it over medium-high heat, add butter and allow it to melt
3. Sauté the onions for 3 minutes
4. Add chopped shrimp with cooled Sautéed onion alongside remaining ingredients listed under stuffing ingredients and transfer to a bowl
5. Cover the mixture and allow it to refrigerate for 60 minutes
6. Rub both sides of the fillet with olive oil
7. Spoon 1/3 cup of the stuffing into the fillet
8. Flatten out the stuffing onto the bottom half of the fillet and fold the Tilapia in half
9. Secure with two toothpicks
10. Dust each fillet with smoked paprika and Old Bay seasoning
11. Preheat your smoker to 400 degrees Fahrenheit
12. Add your preferred wood Pellets and transfer the fillets to a non-stick grill tray
13. Transfer to your smoker and smoker for 30-45 minutes until the internal temperature reaches 145 degrees Fahrenheit
14. Allow the fish to rest for 5 minutes and enjoy!

Nutrition Info: Calories: 620 Fats: 50g Carbs: 6g Fiber: 1g

66. Grilled Shrimp Kabobs

Servings: 4

Cooking Time: 10 Minutes

Ingredients:

- 1 lb. colossal shrimp, peeled and deveined
- 2 tbsp. oil
- 1/2 tbsp. garlic salt
- 1/2 tbsp. salt
- 1/8 tbsp. pepper
- 6 skewers

Directions:

1. Preheat your to 375F.
2. Pat the shrimp dry with a paper towel.

3. In a mixing bowl, mix oil, garlic salt, salt, and pepper
4. Toss the shrimp in the mixture until well coated.
5. Skewer the shrimps and cook in with the lid closed for 4 minutes.
6. Open the lid, flip the skewers, cook for another 4 minutes, or wait until the shrimp is pink and the flesh is opaque.
7. Serve.

Nutrition Info: Calories 325, Total fat 0g, Saturated fat 0g, Total carbs 5g, Net carbs 2g Protein 20g, Sodium 120mg

67. Wood Pellet Grilled Lobster Tail

Servings: 2

Cooking Time: 15 Minutes

Ingredients:

- 10 oz lobster tail
- 1/4 tbsp old bay seasoning
- 1/4 tbsp Himalayan sea salt

- 2 tbsp butter, melted
- 1 tbsp fresh parsley, chopped

Directions:

1. Preheat the wood pellet to 450°F.
2. Slice the tails down the middle using a knife.
3. Season with seasoning and salt, then place the tails on the grill grate.
4. Grill for 15 minutes or until the internal temperature reaches 140°F.
5. Remove the tails and drizzle with butter and garnish with parsley.
6. Serve and enjoy.

Nutrition Info: Calories 305, Total fat 14g, Saturated fat 12g, Total Carbs 10g, Net Carbs 5g, Protein 20g, Sodium: 690mg, Potassium 165mg

68. Buttered Crab Legs

Servings: 4

Cooking Time: 10 Minutes

Ingredients:

- 12 tablespoons butter
- One tablespoon parsley, chopped
- One tablespoon tarragon, chopped
- One tablespoon chives, chopped
- One tablespoon lemon juice
- 4 lb. king crab legs, split in the center

Directions:

1. Set the wood pellet grill to 375 degrees F.
2. Preheat it for 15 minutes while the lid is closed.
3. In a pan over medium heat, simmer the butter, herbs, and lemon juice for 2 minutes.
4. Place the crab legs on the grill.
5. Pour half of the sauce on top.
6. Grill for 10 minutes.
7. Serve with the reserved butter sauce.
8. Tips: You can also use shrimp for this recipe.

69. Citrus Salmon

Servings: 6

Cooking Time: 30 Minutes

Ingredients:

- 2 (1-lb.) salmon fillets
- Salt and freshly ground black pepper, to taste
- 1 tbsp. seafood seasoning
- 2 lemons, sliced
- 2 limes, sliced

Directions:

1. Set the Grill temperature to 225 degrees F and preheat with a closed lid for 15 minutes.
2. Season the salmon fillets with salt, black pepper, and seafood seasoning evenly.
3. Place the salmon fillets onto the grill and top each with lemon and lime slices evenly.

4. Cook for about 30 minutes.

5. Remove the salmon fillets from the grill and serve hot.

Nutrition Info: Calories per serving: 327; Carbohydrates: 1g; Protein: 36.1g; Fat: 19.8g; Sugar: 0.2g; Sodium: 237mg; Fiber: 0.3g

70. Barbecued Scallops

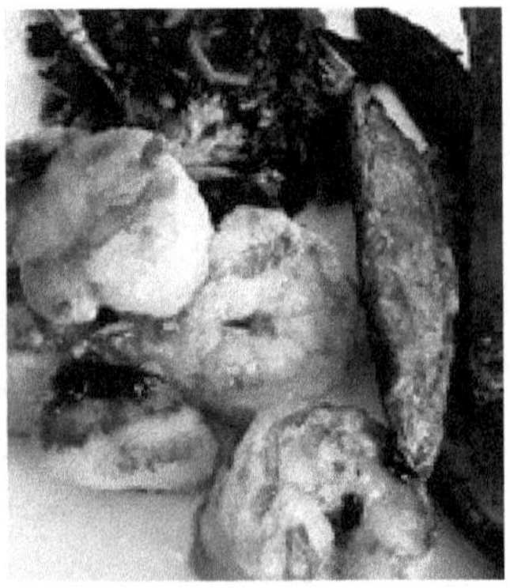

Servings: 4

Cooking Time: 10 Minutes

Ingredients:

- 1 pound large scallops
- 2 tablespoons olive oil
- 1 batch Dill Seafood Rub

Directions:

1. Supply your smoker with wood pellets and follow the manufacturer's specific start-up procedure. Preheat the grill, with the lid closed, to 375°F.

2. Coat the scallops all over with olive oil and season all sides with the rub.
3. Place the scallops directly on the grill grate and grill for 5 minutes per side. Remove the scallops from the grill and serve immediately.

Introduction

Barbeque is a huge part of American cuisine and culture. Smoked meats are a favorite among the entire country. Barbeque becomes a must in summers when families get together on long summer weekends, spending quality time together. Nowadays, this has become nearly impossible because of the tough work-life balance and people's desire to grab an easy bite. No one has the time and energy to set up the conventional-style barbeque. Some people might still be up for doing all the hard work, but most of the population would welcome a quick and easy way to enjoy the smoked flavors of barbequed meat.

Technology has made this difficult feat possible. Electric Smokers are a great appliance that makes our job simple. There was a time when you had to spend the whole day in front of the Smoker to prepare a good smoked steak. With the electric Smoker, you can enjoy the authentic flavor of barbeque with little effort. What the electric Smoker does is that it uses the same conventional method for cooking, but you do not have to do all the hard work manually; the electric Smoker does it for you. All you must do is prepare the meat, set up the electric Smoker, pour in some water in the water tray, throw in some wood chips, turn up the heat according to your needs and set the timer.

Meanwhile, you go about your business, run your errands, have a chat with your friends, and your yummy food is being prepared all on its own. You do not need to worry about temperature control or about managing the charcoal. The electric Smoker fits best with the modern way of life. Another huge advantage of electric smokers, apart from them being super easy to operate, is that they are easy to clean. They are just like little closets which have removable racks. You can remove every part, clean it, and place it back. Also, because the temperature and the smoke can be regulated and controlled, the result is perfect most of the time. The chances for mishaps are rare, unlike the traditional style, where things can get tricky quite often.

If you want to enjoy a delicious barbeque with the least effort, you should read on about this amazing appliance, making you a pro at family barbeques in no time. Enjoy reading!

Chapter 1: What is an Electric Smoker?

In this chapter, the basic introduction and working of the electric Smoker will be discussed. Before understanding the Electric Smoker, we must first understand the meaning of the cooking method that the Electric Smoker uses.

This technique is known as 'Smoking,' and it is a type of process related to barbeque.

71. 1.1. What is Smoking?

Smoking is a more specialized and extreme type of barbecuing. You will be using the smoke from different types of aromatic wood chips or wood chunks in smoking. You may use wood chips of cherry, apple, hickory, mesquite, and many others. These impart their unique flavor and smoky aroma to the meat being smoked.

The process of smoking takes longer than barbecuing. The temperature is also lower than barbecue. The temperature is usually set between 125 to 175°F. The temperature is kept lower because if the temperature is turned up, then the meat's outer layer will be cooked and will not allow the smoke to reach throughout the meat and impart its rich aroma and taste.

Smoking is an advanced technique, and it required a much longer time for food preparation than grilling and normal barbeque. This method also requires a maximum amount of expertise to understand the texture of different types of meat and how they will be perfectly smoked.

1.2 The Electric Smoker

An electric smoker is a cooking appliance that is used outside. Smoking is an advanced type of variation of barbecue. The electric Smoker uses an electric source and heating rods to produce heat for cooking and smoking. The conventional way to smoke is to burn charcoal to produce the required heat, but the electric Smoker is easier to use and simple to operate. The whole process is cleaner as compared to the conventional style. The body of the electric Smoker is either made of stainless steel or cast iron.

(An electric smoker)

There are numerous different types of electric smokers available in the market. You have an option to choose a smoker that is according to your requirements. Different models vary in their specific features, size, number of cooking racks present, temperature control features, number of cycles, preheat options, keep warm option, manual settings, automatic settings, digital displays, and control panels.

Sometimes variety can also overwhelm a buyer. To buy an electric smoker, it is recommended to first determine your requirements and then research the market too but the proper kind of Smoker for yourself. In the following pages, you will also find guidelines to help you decide whether you even need an electric smoker or not. Before that, we will briefly discuss the common features present in almost all electric smokers.

1.3 Working of an Electric Smoker

Normally, when you see an electric smoker, it looks like a cabinet; it is quite efficient in smoking the meat with relatively few components. The basic heating function is that the electric rods heat the entire cooking chamber, and the heated air is spread throughout the chamber. This causes the meat to cook by convection. There are six basic components of the electric Smoker:

- Cooking Chamber
- Woodchip tray
- Electric Heating rods or other heating elements
- Racks or grills to place the meat.
- Water Pan

1.3.1 Cooking Chamber

Like the gas smokers and the charcoal smokers, the electric smokers also have a vertical alignment. The space designated for cooking is at the top. The electric heating rods are placed at the bottom of the cooking chamber. Above the heating, rods are the grills, wood chips drawer and the water pan.

1.3.2 Electric Heating Rods:

The electric rods are placed at the base of the electric Smoker. They are the main source of heat for cooking. Some models of the electric Smoker have one heating rod, and some have more than one rods. This depends on the shape and size of the electric Smoker.

1.3.3 Wood Chip Tray

This is a specific space or tray provided above the electric rods to place the wood chips or wood chunks within the heating chamber. When the woodchips burn slowly, they cause smoke, which spreads within the cooking chamber and surrounds the meat. This smoke gives the meat a smoky and rich flavor. The woodchip tray is sometimes called the firebox as well.

Different types of hardwood are available to put in the electric Smoker. You can use various wood chips and chunks of mesquite, oak, alder, apple, cherry, maple, and hickory.

1.3.4 Water Pan

This is like a slightly deep pan or tray, fixed like a rack in the electric Smoker. Before starting the Smoker, this tray is filled with cold water. The main function is that when the heating rods are turned on, this cold water keeps the temperature from rising quickly inside the heating chamber. The other function is that steam is created when the water is heated up to a boiling point, which helps cook the meat. The steam helps the convection cooking process.

1.3.5 Grills or Racks

Above the water, the tray has placed the racks or grills. These are made of stainless steel. The food is placed on these for cooking. You can put the meat directly on the grill, or you can use heatproof skillets or barbecue utensils.

1.3.6 Vents and Dampers

the vents are usually placed at the top part of the electric Smoker. When the Smoker's temperature gets too high, the vents are opened to release some hot air and bring the temperature down.

The dampers are there for exactly the opposite reason. They are placed at the bottom part of the electric Smoker. When you open the dampers, oxygen enters the cooking chamber. The flames of the woodchips feed on this oxygen and increase the temperature inside the chamber.

Chapter 2. Why buy an Electric Smoker?

If you are someone who loves barbecue and the rich flavor of smoked meat, you might have thought about investing in an electric smoker. Even though you think about it, you are not quite sure whether you should invest in an electric smoker or not. You cannot deny that it is an expensive appliance and if you only occasionally barbecue, this appliance is not for you. Having said that, if you enjoy preparing delicious barbecue now and then, you might want to consider the electric Smoker. Using an electric smoker is easier than the conventional barbeque method, and it is much easier to clean. If you enjoy the smoky aroma and taste in each bite of meat, you might want to ditch the conventional method and adopt electric smoking. This is perfect for that tender, aromatic, and rich smoke flavor. However, you must be warned against the prejudice that surrounds electric smokers. The die-heart conventional barbecue community may argue that the electric Smoker does not give off the meat's authentic smoky flavor. You may agree or not to this argument but investing in an electric smoker would be your best bet if you are new to smoking.

In this chapter, we will discuss the top five reasons to buy an electric smoker. The five arguments in favor of the electric Smoker are:

- Perfect choice for beginners
- The cost
- The easy usage
- You can set it up where conventional barbeque grills might not be allowed.
- The option to cold smoke

72. 2.1. Perfect Choice for Beginners

Investing in an electric smoker is a safe choice for beginners. Smoking is a slightly tricky technique. If you go by the conventional way, it might take you longer to learn and maybe you might give up early on. With the electric Smoker, you can operate it with ease. The temperature and length of cooking can be regulated, and the best part is that the results are almost always perfect. Getting perfect results in cooking is a huge plus because it further motivates you.

Using the electric Smoker, you can learn and become familiar with the basic method and technique involved. Once you have learned the basics, you can either move on to the more conventional style or even decide to stick to the electric Smoker.

73. 2.2. The Cost

If you survey the market, you will find that electric smokers are cheaper than their conventional counterparts. When you look closely, the amount of food they can cook in one session is quite commendable. Another reason the electric Smoker might feel more appealing is that it needs only a one-time setup. After the initial setup, no maintenance is required. Cleaning is easy. To operate is easy. So, in the long run, this seems to be a better investment.

74. 2.3. The Easy Usage

If you see the conventional system of smoking and barbecue, you have a lot to manage. You must control the optimum temperature, need the expertise to light the charcoal, maintain airflow to keep a smooth temperature and manage any temperature spikes or accidents during the entire procedure. In short, you will be on your toes the whole time. Now, flip the situation to the electric Smoker. You prepare your food items, place them on the grills, fill in the water tray, put them in the woodchips, and turn on the heating rods. You can even set the time. It is as easy as this. In case you are hosting a few people over, you will have plenty of time to set up the area and interact with your guests.

75. 2.4. Can Carry the Electric Smoker Anywhere with Power Supply

The appliance comes in handy in two situations. Many states have a fire ban in summers, meaning you cannot set up a charcoal grill or do any cooking outside. There is a fear of forest fires due to the dry summer air. You can take out your electric Smoker and enjoy proper smoked food with friends and family in such a situation.

Another situation where the electric Smoker comes in handy is in small houses and apartments where space is an issue. In apartments, there is a prohibition on barbequing and smoke. You can easily set up your electric Smoker on your balcony and enjoy your favorite food in this situation.

76. 2.5. The Option to Cold Smoke

Sometimes you want to cold smoke some food items like cheese and bacon. It is not easily possible on conventional smokers. It would help if you bought the cold smoke attachments with an electric smoker, generally available easily with all-electric smoker models. This attachment can be used to prepare a variety of preparations like meatloaves, deserts, dried meat, and fish sausages.

Chapter 3. Proper Usage of the Electric Smoker

After you have purchased the Electric Smoker, comes to the process of setting it up. Most electric smokers are easy to install and setup. It is best to read the manual to understand the working of the specific model.

This chapter will discuss step-by-step how we should prepare our food items and the correct method and sequence to smoke our desired food product.

77. 3.1. Preparation of Meat

The meat preparation will be done the same way you would do for conventional barbecue and smoking as usual. Some people follow their family recipes passed down through generations. Some people prefer a marinade kept overnight; some perform a dry rub to season and prepare the meat. It is entirely up to you how you want to season the meat you want to prepare. The electric Smoker can smoke every kind of meat, so do not be shy and prepare your favorite meat for smoking. Be sure that the electric Smoker will prepare the same flavor and texture you expect from the traditional style smoker will give.

78. 3.2. Setting up the Electric Smoker

Few points should be kept in mind when setting up the electric Smoker. The first and most important is that this is an outdoor appliance. Please keep it in a properly ventilated space. It cannot be kept indoors. It must be set up outside. It should be set up on a flat and strong surface that can withstand high temperatures. Sometimes the appliance can heat-up up to high temperatures. Please keep it in an open space with room to move about so that the appliance is in no danger to be tripped over and become a hazard. Keep children away from the electric Smoker while operating and afterward until it cools down after one or two hours.

79. 3.3. Read the Electric Smoker Manual

Different models of Electric Smokers have a different set of instructions. The basic working of thee the Electric Smokers is the same, but there is a slight difference in how each Smoker is operated. It would help if you had a complete understanding of how your appliance is turned on and off, how to regulate temperature, when is it safe to open the appliance, what temperatures are suitable for which meat, how much time it requires for specific meats. It will help if you read up about all such details to use your Electric Smoker to its fullest.

80. 3.4. Seasoning the Electric Smoker

This is an important process. You only need to do this once when your electric Smoker is brand new. To get rid of any harmful chemicals left in the Smoker during manufacturing, this procedure is done. All manuals have detailed descriptions of the seasoning. You must follow the exact instructions of your Electric Smoker because they are model specific.

However, a common procedure followed for seasoning is that you apply any cooking oil on all the electric Smoker's inner surfaces such that the surfaces are completely coated. Now turn on the Electric Smoker and let it operate empty for 2 to 3 hours. Then let it cook, and then your appliance is ready for use.

81. 3.5. Preparing the Cooking Chamber

First, make sure that the cooking chamber is clean. Fill the water tray with water. This must be done before turning on the heat. Fill in the wood chip tray with wood chips or woodchucks that you wish to use. Usually, the wood chip compartment should be filled if the meat will be smoked for 3 to 4 hours. Next, set up the temperature and time for smoking. Always remember that the heating chamber should be preheated. Do not put the meat in the cold chamber and turn on the heat afterward. It is always recommended to put the meat in a well-heated chamber. This is a pro tip for the best results.

82. 3.6. Putting in the meat

First, let the cooking chamber reach a certain temperature, then place the meat on the grills. You will need to open the chamber, place the meat, and then close it. Take care of that you put in the meat swiftly so that less heat is lost from within the chamber during this action. Temperature and the correct amount of heat are essential for the meat to be prepared to perfection. It is also recommended not to open the chamber when the meat is being smoked. This might disrupt the smoking process and bring the temperature down. The same rule applies to smoking as the one that applies in baking. Optimum temperature is essential.

83. 3.7. The Process of Smoking

This is a slow process. It usually takes three or more hours. Only fish takes a shorter while to smoke. Otherwise, all other meats take much longer. Always take care to replenish the woodchips during the smoking process.

The smoking process will be carried out on its own, so there will be no other precaution except for keeping an eye on the wood chips.

Another thing to look out for will be the water. This water serves as the steam that gives the meats the required moisture that does not let them dry out. If the water is dried up, the meat will also become dry and difficult to chew on. So, it is always important that there is enough moisture circulation in the heating chamber. Always keep an eye out for the water tray. It should not be dry.

84. 3.8. Taking out the meat

Before taking out the meat from the heated chamber, always check if the meat is cooked properly. Every meat has an internal temperature that indicates its doneness. So before bringing the meat out, insert the thermometer to the thickest part of the meat can see that the optimum temperature has been achieved or not. If you think the meat is undercooked, keep it in the chamber for 20 more minutes and check again. If all seems well, take out the Smoker's rack and place it on the counter to let it rest and then slice your meat.

Serve the meat with traditional side dishes like coleslaw, corn on the cob or baked potatoes. With the electric Smoker, you do not need to worry about the meat not being cooked properly. With the temperature regulation, the chance for accidents is reduced significantly.

Chapter 4. Tips and Tricks to Smoke Anything

Knowing some tricks and hacks about appliances always helps in preparing perfect meals. The same is the case with an electric smoker. This chapter discusses a few tricks and tips to help you in preparing smoked meats and foods. Usually, we start learning with experience but learning from other's experiences can give you a head start. Here is a list of tried and tested tricks and tips for the usage of an Electric Smoker. These tips and tricks will help you along your journey with the electric Smoker. Read all the points carefully to get the best results.

85. 4.1. Do not Over Smoke the Food

When you first buy an electric smoker, you might be tempted to use many strong aromatic woodchips. But the reality is that you do not need an overpowering smoke flavor to make the barbecue delicious; only a mild smoky flavor will do the job. It is also true for poultry that over-smoked chicken becomes bitter and inedible. So always be careful about the amount of smoke you want for your food. In the case of smoke, the less is more saying is true.

86. 4.2. Smoke Chicken at High Temperature

Chicken is not one of those meat groups which need a lower temperature for a longer time to be perfectly cooked. The chicken cooks at a higher temperature. The rule of thumb is to take the temperature to 275◦F and smoke the chicken for around one to two hours. To check the chicken for doneness, insert a probe inside the chicken thigh and see that the internal temperature is about 165◦F. The proper cooking of chicken is important because undercooked chicken can cause harmful effects and infections to the body.

87. 4.3. Do not Soak the Wood Chips

It is common practice to soak woodchips in water before use. What happens is that when we soak the wood chips and put them in the Smoker and the smoking starts, white smoke is created. We think that this white smoke gives a smoky, rich flavor to the meat, but it is not true. This white smoke is just steam that dilutes the smoke's flavor and interferes with the temperature inside the chamber.

What you should do is that use the wood chips directly. The smoke that will be created will be thin blue smoke, which is the type of smoke that imparts a rich aromatic flavor to the smoked dishes.

88. 4.4. Season your Electric Smoker before Use

This point is more of a health concern rather than a tip or trick. Seasoning is the process performed before cooking anything in the Smoker. This is usually done to eliminate all factory residue, chemicals, and dust from inside the cavity that has been left over from the manufacturing plant.

This process also has a good effect on subsequent smoking as well. After the seasoning, a black layer of smoke is formed on the electric Smoker's inner surfaces. So, after seasoning, whatever you will smoke, the black coating will impart the smoky flavor.

89. 4.5. Preheat the Cooking Chamber

Always preheat the cooking chamber. Turn on the electric heat rods before putting in the meat and wait till the optimum temperature is reached; only then should you put in the meat. This will ensure that the meat will neither remain undercooked or overcooked.

90. 4.6. Put Poultry in Oven to Finish

Most of the electric smokers have a maximum temperature of 275◦F. This temperature is enough to cook poultry to perfection, but the desired crispy skins cannot be achieved at this temperature. So, if you want crispy skins, take out the chicken from the Smoker and place it in the oven at around 300◦F for 10 minutes. You will have yummy crispy skins.

91. 4.7. Cover the Racks and Grills with Aluminum Foil

This tip is more for cleanliness than the taste of the smoked good. It would help if you covered all your racks and trays with aluminum foil. This will protect the racks and grills, and whenever the aluminum gets dirty, it can be replaced with a fresh layer of aluminum foil.

92. 4.8. Do not use the Wood Chip Tray

In the electric Smoker, you fill the wood tray with woodchips. Often, people have experienced that they must refill the wood chip tray repeatedly, and it can be a bit inconvenient. Rather than wood chips, you can use a pellet smoker. A pellet smoker is a separately available tube that gives off thin blue smoke, which gives the aroma and amazing flavor to the smoked meats.

93. 4.9. Leave the Vent Open

It is a good idea to keep the vent of the Electric Smoker completely open. This is to prevent the accumulation of creosote. Creosote is a substance in smoke that gives a smoky flavor to the foods. This substance is good to impart a smoky flavor to the dish, but a high quantity of this substance can accumulate over the meat and gives off a bitter flavor.

94. 4.10. Control the Temperature Swings

The temperature swings are phenomena that are seen in all heating appliances using heating rods. What happens is that if you set the temperature of the appliance at 220◦F, the rod, when it reaches this temperature, will turn off; however, the temperature still keeps rising and is risen to about 240◦F and then starts coming back, it gets lower and lower about 210◦F, and then the rods turn on again, and it takes a while to get to 220◦F. you need to learn to manage this situation by keeping the temperature selection about 10◦F lower than the desired temperature. This way, the temperature swings will be controlled.

95. 4.11. Invest in a Good Thermometer

In smoking, you can often be confused if the meat is done or not. Sometimes you can be fooled but the appliance's internal thermostat. But the doneness of meat is determined by the internal temperature of the meat. So, to check the internal temperature of the meat, you should have a separate thermometer. Such thermometers are commonly known as probes. You can insert the probe into the thickest part of the meat and determine the internal temperature. We must understand that the thermostat of the electric Smoker and the meat's internal temperature are different, and the doneness of the meat depends on the meat's internal temperature. Different meats have the different internal temperature that determines that they are fully cooked. Some meats are done at lower internal temperatures, such as fish and seafood. Some meats require high temperatures, like beef and lamb. Understanding this is especially important, and the first step towards this understanding is investing in a good thermometer.

96. 4.12. Keep the Meat Overnight Before Smoking

To achieve the meat's full flavors, it is always a good idea to keep the meat overnight. It does not matter if you decide to marinate, dry rub, or brine the meat; leaving it in the refrigerator overnight will cause the flavors to fully absorb in the meat, and the meat will also become tender before smoking. The meat will be cooked even if you decide not to let it stay overnight, but the results might not be as good as the meat that has been kept overnight. In smoking and barbecue, patience plays an important role. The more patient you are, the better your food will cook and taste.

97. 4.13. Do not Hurry.

Smoking is a long process. It takes time for meats to properly smoke. Whenever you decide to smoke meat, always keep in mind that you must have the patience to let the meat cook completely. Sometimes the temptation to check on our dishes can be harmful to the recipe. When you open the electric smoker door, the temperature is disrupted, and the recipe might be affected. Even opening the door for one or two minutes can even have such an effect. So, you must be patient while the Smoker is working. This is an amazing appliance, and you should trust it to work its wonder. All you must do is sit back and relax.

Chapter 5. Ultimate Electric Smoker Recipes

In this chapter, you will find easy-to-follow recipes that you can make in your Electric Smoker. You must follow all recipes exactly according to the instructions for the best results.

98. 5.1. Beef BBQ Brisket

This is an easy recipe for BBQ brisket that you will prepare in your Electric Smoker. Be assured that you will enjoy the original BBQ flavor. The meat will have a beautiful texture on the outside and will be tender inside. Just follow the instructions carefully, and you are in for a treat. They this recipe and you will not be disappointed.

- Course: Dinner

- Cuisine: American BBQ
- Total Time: 8 hours 50 minutes
- Preparation Time: 30 minutes
- Cooking Time: 8 hours
- Rest Time: 20 minutes
- Serving Size: 2 servings
- Nutritional Value Per Serving
    - Calories: 564 calories
    - Carbohydrates: 0 g
    - Protein: 77.3 g
    - Fats: 27.4 g

Equipment Used:

- Electric Smoker

Ingredients:

1. BBQ rub (store-bought) 5 tbsp.
2. Beef Brisket ½ kg.

Instructions:

- Preheat the electric Smoker at 225°F.
- Then prepare the beef brisket. Wash the meat and pat it dry.
- Trim all the excess fat from the brisket, leaving only one-fourth of an inch of fat on the meat.
- Next, remove the excess skin from the underside of the meat cut.
- Now, apply the BBQ rub on the beef on both sides generously.

- Put the brisket in the Electric Smoker and insert the probe in the thickest part of the beef.
- Smoke the beef until the temperature has reached 160◦F. This usually takes six hours. It might take longer, so you must see when the temperature reaches a certain point.
- At this stage, please take out the brisket very carefully and wrap it tightly in aluminum foil.
- Place it back into the Smoker and wait until the brisket's temperature reaches 190◦F. This usually takes additional 2 hours. The time might be a bit more depending on the brisket.
- When the beef is at 190◦F, take it out of the Smoker.
- Let it rest for 20 to 30 minutes.
- Then unwrap the brisket and slice it.
- Enjoy the delicious BBQ brisket.

5.2. Smoked Salmon

The best thing about this recipe is that it is easy to make and quick to prepare. Minimum ingredients are used to achieve perfection with this smoked salmon. Try this recipe, and you will be in for a mouthwatering treat.

- Course: Lunch
- Cuisine: American
- Total Time: 2 hours 10 minutes
- Preparation Time: 10 minutes
- Cooking Time: 1 hour
- Rest: 20 minutes
- Serving Size: 3 servings
- Nutritional Value Per Serving
    - Calories: 454 calories
    - Carbohydrates: 0 g
    - Protein: 57.5 g
    - Fats: 24.2 g

Equipment Used:

- Electric Smoker

Ingredients:

1. Fresh Salmon 1 kg.

2. Brown Sugar 2 tbsp
3. Dried Dill 1 tsp
4. Pepper 1 tsp
5. Salt 1tsp

Instructions:

- Wash and pat dry the fish carefully. You must be careful with raw fish meat because it is delicate and can break.
- Mix the salt, pepper, sugar, and dill in a bowl.
- Rub this sugar mixture on the top side of the fish.
- Put it in the refrigerator for one hour. This will allow the fish to dry brine.
- Preheat the Electric Smoker at 250◦F.
- Place a probe into the thickest part of the meat.
- Let it smoke until the meat reaches 145◦F. It takes about 45 minutes to one hour.
- The dish can be served at room temperature or even cold.
- For this specific dish, you can use pecan, cherry, or oak wood for a subtle flavor.

5.3. Smoked Chicken

Chicken is one of the most widely popular food throughout the world. This recipe gives smoked chicken a spicy and flavorful twist. The brown sugar used in the rub gives it a caramelized look and texture and adds richness to the taste. Try this recipe out and you will not be disappointed.

- Course: Dinner
- Cuisine: American BBQ
- Total Time: 5 hours
- Preparation Time: 30 minutes
- Cooking Time: 4 hours
- Rest Time: 30 minutes
- Serving Size: 4 servings
- Nutritional Value Per Serving
    - Calories: 240 calories
    - Carbohydrates: 0 g
    - Protein: 21 g
    - Fats: 17 g

Equipment Used:

- Electric Smoker

Ingredients:

1. Medium sized whole chicken with skin

2. Thyme 1 tbsp
3. Cayenne Pepper 2 tbsp
4. Garlic Powder 1 tbsp
5. Chili Powder 2 tbsp
6. Salt 1 tbsp
7. Sugar 2 tbsp
8. Onion Powder 1 tbsp
9. Black Pepper 2 tbsp
10. Olive Oil 3 tbsp

Instructions:

- Arrange the woodchips in the electric smoker tray. You can use peach, apple, or cherry woodchips. Then turn on the electric Smoker to preheat at 225◦F.
- In a medium-sized mixing bowl, mix the thyme, cayenne pepper, garlic powder, chili powder, salt, sugar, onion powder, and black pepper. This will make the perfect rub for the chicken.
- First, rub the whole chicken with olive oil. All sides and inside the hollow cavity of chicken as well.
- After that, apply the prepared rub on the chicken generously. Rub it on the entire surface of the chicken.
- Put the skin over the breast of the chicken and apply the rub under the skin as well.
- Put the prepared chicken in the electric Smoker and insert a probe in the thigh.
- Check the chicken after every hour and take it out when the meat's internal temperature reaches 164◦F. The whole process takes about 4 hours.

- Served the smoked chicken warm.

5.4. Smoked Corn on the Cob

Corn on the cob is a crowd's favorite side dish. It is popular among kids and adults alike. These complement all sorts of meats in a barbecue and give us that much-needed light and sweet flavors in the middle of a high protein barbecue. Try this easy recipe, and you will not regret preparing some smoked corn on the cob.

- Course: Side Dish

- Cuisine: American
- Total Time: 5 hours 10 minutes
- Preparation Time: 4 hours
- Cooking Time: 1 hour
- Rest Time: 10 minutes
- Serving Size: 6 servings
- Nutritional Value Per Serving
    - Calories: 142 calories
    - Carbohydrates: 16.6 g
    - Protein: 2.7 g
    - Fats: 8.6 g

Equipment Used:

- Electric Smoker

Ingredients:

1. Ear corn with husks 6 pieces
2. Brown sugar 2 tbsp
3. Salt ½ tsp
4. Garlic powder ½ tsp
5. Melted butter ¼ cup.
6. Onion powder 1 tsp
7. Sliced green onion 3 pieces.

Instructions:

- Take a large roasting pot and fill it half with room temperature water.

- Pull the husks of all the corn cobs and remove the silks. Let the husks remain attached to the cob but just pulled back.
- Soak the corn cobs in the water and if needed, fill the pot with more water to completely immerse the cobs into water.
- Soak for 4 hours.
- After that remove, the cobs from the pot and place them on paper towels and let them dry.
- Preheat the electric Smoker at 225°F. Place the woodchips inside the electric Smoker.
- In a mixing bowl, mix the butter, sugar, salt, onion powder, and garlic powder to make a rub for the corn on the cob.
- With the help of a brush, apply the rub generously to the corn cobs.
- Pull the husks back on the corn cobs. Place them in the electric Smoker.
- Leave for 60 minutes and then take them out.
- Let them rest for 10 minutes, and then serve them as a delicious side dish.

5.5. Grilled Chicken Thighs with Asparagus

This delicious chicken recipe is perfect for enjoying on the weekend. It is easy to make and takes only 2 hours to prepare. The juicy chicken with the light smokiness is a success with kids and adults alike. This dish will be a crowd favorite. Try out this recipe and enjoy it with friends and family.

- Course: Lunch
- Cuisine: American
- Total Time: 5 hours
- Preparation Time: 3 hours
- Cooking Time: 2 hours
- Rest Time: 10 minutes
- Serving Size: 3 servings
- Nutritional Value Per Serving
    - Calories: 482 calories
    - Carbohydrates: 58.8 g
    - Protein: 58.5 g
    - Fats: 19.3 g

Equipment Used:

- Electric Smoker

Ingredients:

For Chicken:

1. Chicken thighs 3 to 4 pieces
2. Store-bought BBQ rub 5 tbsp.
3. Water as required.
4. Sugar 1 tsp
5. Salt 1 tsp
6. ¼ cup apple cider vinegar

For Asparagus

1. Asparagus 1 bunch
2. Red pepper flakes 1 tsp
3. Balsamic Vinegar ¼ cup
4. Pepper 1 tsp
5. Salt 1 tsp

Equipment Used:

- Electric Smoker

Instructions:

- Prepare to brine the chicken thighs. Put the chicken in a large zip lock bag, then add Vinegar, salt, and sugar.
- Then, fill the bag with water such that the chicken pieces are completely soaked. Put it in the refrigerator for 2 to 3 hours.

- The brining process will ensure that the chicken does not dry out while in the electric Smoker.
- Similarly, prepare a marinade for the asparagus bunch as well. Please put it in a large zip lock bag. Add the balsamic vinegar, salt pepper, pepper flakes and water to soak the asparagus. Please leave it in the refrigerator for 3 hours.
- Prepare a small BBQ spray bottle having one part vinegar, two parts water and 1 tsp sugar. Mix it properly. This will be used to spray on the chicken while it is being smoked.
- Take the chicken out of the refrigerator after 2 hours and wash and dry the pieces.
- Apply the BBQ rub generously on the chicken pieces.
- Preheat the electric Smoker at 225◦F for 15 minutes. Put the apple woodchips in the wood tray.
- Place the chicken thighs in the electric Smoker.
- Spray with the BBQ spray bottle after every 20 to 30 minutes. This will prevent the chicken from drying.
- Smoke the chicken for about two hours.
- Take the chicken out of the Smoker and let it rest for 10 minutes.
- Meanwhile, please take out the asparagus and spread it on a paper towel and pat dry.
- Put the asparagus in the electric Smoker and leave for 10 minutes, and then take it out.
- Serve the chicken with a side of asparagus.
- This is a good pairing to serve, and the asparagus complements the smoked chicken beautifully.

99. 5.6. Smoked Turkey Breast

Turkey has often been bland and boring meat. This recipe gives the turkey a tasty and spicy twist. The BBQ sauce mixed with hot sauce and honey gives the smoked turkey a rich flavor and an amazing texture. Try out this mouthwatering and delicious recipe and enjoy the aromatic and tender turkey meat. This recipe never disappoints.

- Course: Lunch
- Cuisine: American
- Total Time: 3 hours 20 minutes
- Preparation Time: 5 minutes
- Cooking Time: 3 hours
- Resting Time: 10 minutes

- Serving Size: 3 to 4 servings
- Nutritional Value Per Serving
    - Calories: 380 calories
    - Carbohydrates: 16.5 g
    - Protein: 28.2 g
    - Fats: 20.8 g

Equipment Used:

- Electric Smoker

Ingredients:

1. Turkey breast 1 piece
2. Store-bought BBQ rub 4 tbsp.
3. Olive oil 3 tbsp.
4. Butter 100 g
5. Hot Tabasco sauce 2 tsp
6. Honey 1tsp

Instructions:

- First, preheat the electric Smoker at 250◦F for at least 15 minutes.
- Put in the mesquite woodchips in the Smoker.
- Next, prepare the turkey meat. Cover the whole meat with a layer of olive oil. Rub the oil generously.
- Then apply the BBQ rub on the whole meat piece. Rub the mixture generously so that the whole turkey breast is covered with the BBQ rub.

- In a heatproof cup, prepare the basting mixture for the turkey. Add the butter, cut into small cubes to the cup. Put in the honey, hot sauce and ¼ teaspoon BBQ rub.
- Put the turkey and the cup in the electric Smoker and let it remain closed for approximately 45 minutes. Put a probe in the turkey meat at the thickest part of the meat.
- When you open the electric Smoker after 45 minutes, you will see that the basting mixture is prepared and is steaming.
- Pour the basting mixture about 2 tbsp on the meat and let it smoke.
- Repeat the procedure with the basting mixture after every 20 minutes.
- When the internal temperature of meat is near 170◦F, raise the electric Smoker's heat to 270◦F for the last 10 minutes.
- Take out the meat when the internal temperature reaches 170◦F.
- Let the meat rest for 15 minutes and then slice it.
- Serve this mouthwatering and delicious meal to your friends and family.

5.7. Smoked Potatoes

Baked potatoes are an all-time favorite side dish. They go well with all meats, especially chicken. They can be served as it is or with a rich sour cream. This is an easy and useful recipe to smoke potatoes perfectly. This recipe is simple and easy to prepare and goes well with almost anything. You can even make this and have it on its own. It is great comfort food. Try it out and you will not be disappointed.

- Course: Side Dish
- Cuisine: American
- Total Time: 2 hours 20 minutes
- Preparation Time: 10 minutes
- Cooking Time: 2 hours
- Rest Time: 10 minutes
- Serving Size: 4 servings
- Nutritional Value Per Serving
    - Calories: 119 calories
    - Carbohydrates: 10 g
    - Protein: 1.8 g
    - Fats: 8.5 g

Equipment Used:

- Electric Smoker

Ingredients:

1. Medium sized potatoes 4 pieces
2. Olive oil ¼ cup
3. Granular Salt ¾ cup

Instructions:

- Preheat the electric Smoker at 275◦F. Put in the wood chips of your choice. Preheat for at least 15 minutes.
- Wash the potatoes and dry them on a paper towel.
- Poke each potato with a fork 5 or six times at different places on the potato surface. This will prevent the potato from exploding when it is exposed to a high temperature in the electric Smoker.
- Pour the oil in an open cup and coat each potato with a thin layer of oil.
- Next, pour the salt into a shallow dish. Coat the potatoes with this salt.
- Place the potatoes in the electric Smoker and wait for approximately 2 hours.
- After 2 hours, check the potatoes for doneness. The potatoes should be cooked and soft.
- Take the potatoes out and let them rest for 10 minutes.
- Slit the potatoes from the entrance and fill them with American-style chili if you want to serve as a main dish.
- Another serving idea is to slit the center and fill it with sour cream and top it with sliced green onions. This makes a perfect side dish.

5.8. Smoked Burgers

Burgers are a staple food in American cuisine. These smoked beef burgers have a smoky flavor and are perfect for a quiet weekend lunch with the family. The burgers do not have a sauce but are still delicious and mouthwatering. The best part about this recipe is that it is easy to make, and it takes less time for preparation and cooking. Try this recipe and enjoy it with friends and family.

- Course: Lunch
- Cuisine: American
- Total Time: 1 hour 20 minutes
- Preparation Time: 10 minutes
- Cooking Time: 1 hour

- Rest Time: 10 minutes
- Serving Size: 6 servings
- Nutritional Value Per Serving
    - Calories: 160 calories
    - Carbohydrates: 1 g
    - Protein: 11 g
    - Fats: 11 g

Equipment Used:

- Electric Smoker

Ingredients:

1. Pre-prepared beef burger patties 6 pieces
2. Salt 2 tbsp
3. Garlic Powder ½ tbsp
4. Pepper 1 tbsp
5. Dehydrated onion ½ tbsp

Instructions:

- Make sure that the burger patties are at room temperature.
- In a mixing bowl, add the salt, pepper, garlic powder, and dehydrated onion. Mix these ingredients well such that a rub is formed.
- Apply this rub on the burger patties. Cover both sides of the burger patty with the rub.
- Preheat the electric Smoker at 275°F for 15 minutes. Add the woodchips to the electric Smoker.

- Next, place the burger patties in the Electric Smoker.
- If you want your burger to be medium-well done, smoke for 45 minutes and if you want it to be well done, smoke for 60 minutes. This depends entirely on your preference.
- Once the patties are cooked, take them out of the Smoker and let them rest for 10 minutes.
- Next, prepare the buns and put them in the burger patties. These can be served as it is or some raw vegetables and sauce can be added.

5.9. Smoked Chicken Drumsticks

This is a recipe for mouthwatering and flavorful drumsticks. The flavors are sweet and spicy. This recipe is prepared in 2 ½ hours, and you can enjoy these tasty drumsticks with BBQ sauce. Do try this recipe; this is a hit among kids and adults alike.

- Course: Dinner
- Cuisine: American
- Total Time: 3 hours

- Preparation Time: 15 minutes
- Cooking Time: 2 hours 30 minutes
- Serving Size: 6 persons
- Nutritional Value Per Serving
    - Calories: 180 calories
    - Carbohydrates: 8 g
    - Protein: 17 g
    - Fats: 8 g

Equipment Used:

- Electric Smoker

Ingredients:

1. Chicken Drumsticks 1.5 kg.
2. Store-bought Steak Rub ½ cup.
3. Cayenne Pepper 1 tsp
4. BBQ sauce ½ cup
5. Tabasco sauce 5 tbsp

Instructions:

- Wash and pat dry the drumsticks.
- Do not remove the skins from the chicken drumsticks.
- Rub the drumsticks with the store-bought steak rub and the cayenne pepper. Keep the drumsticks in the refrigerator for 2 hours.
- After a while, prepare the Electric Smoker.
- Put in the apple woodchips for a mild smoky flavor.

- Fill in the water tray with cold water.
- Turn on the electric Smoker at 250◦F to preheat.
- In the meanwhile, arrange the drumsticks in a stainless-steel wings rack.
- Put in the drumsticks in the Smoker and leave for 2 hours.
- At the end of 2 hours, check the internal temperature of drumsticks. The drumsticks are ready when the thermometer shows 160◦F as the internal temperature of the meat.
- Take out the drumsticks and let them rest for 5 minutes.
- Meanwhile, mix the BBQ sauce and tabasco sauce in a bowl.
- Dip all the drumsticks in the sauce one by one and arrange them on a platter.
- Serve hot.

5.10. Smoked Mac and Cheese

Mac and cheese as comfortable as comfort foods get. It serves as a great side dish with your barbeque. It is conventionally made in an oven, but you can also use a smoker to prepare this dish to give an extra smoky richness.

- Course: Side Dish
- Cuisine: American
- Total Time: 2 hours 30 minutes
- Preparation Time: 30 minutes
- Cooking Time: 2 hours
- Serving Size: 4 servings
- Nutritional Value Per Serving
    - Calories: 380 calories
    - Carbohydrates: 50 g
    - Protein: 8 g
    - Fats: 4 g

Equipment Used:

Electric Smoker

Ingredients:

1. Elbow Macaroni 1 packet, about ½ kg
2. Milk 3 cups
3. Flour ¼ cup
4. Cheese of your choice (grated) 500 g.
5. Cream cheese 250 g
6. Butter ¼ cup
7. Salt to taste
8. Pepper to taste

Instructions:

- First, boil 12 cups of water in a medium cooking pot. When the water comes to a boil, add the elbow macaroni, and let it boil for 8 to 10 minutes. When the macaroni is boiled, remove all the water, and put the macaroni aside.
- Next, you will prepare the cheese sauce.
- In a medium-sized pan, put in the butter in melt it over the flame. After the butter is melted, add the flour, and mix it. Cook for about two minutes till the flour starts to brown.
- Next, add the milk and cook for five minutes with constant stirring or whisking to not form lumps. Let the milk thicken. When the milk starts to thicken, take the saucepan off the flame, and add cream cheese.
- Mix the cream cheese and make a smooth mixture.
- In a heat-resistant bowl, add the cheese. Pour this mixture over the cheese and mix well.

- At this point, prepare the electric Smoker and put it to preheat at 225∘F.
- Now take an aluminum tray and spread the cooked macaroni in its base.
- Pour the cream and cheese mixture over the macaroni such that it is fully immersed in the mixture.
- Put the aluminum tray in the Smoker for two hours.
- Take out the dish after two hours. The upper layer will come out crusty with cheesy and gooey richness beneath.
- Enjoy your mac and cheese separately or with barbequed chicken or meat.

5.11. BBQ Smoked Ribs

If you are someone who enjoys the ribs on the bone, this recipe is just for you. You will enjoy the rich smokiness of the ribs flavored with mild herbs served with BBQ sauce. Preparing BBQ ribs might be a bit tricky if you go the conventional way, but the ribs prepared in the electric Smoker save you all the hassle, giving you the same flavor.

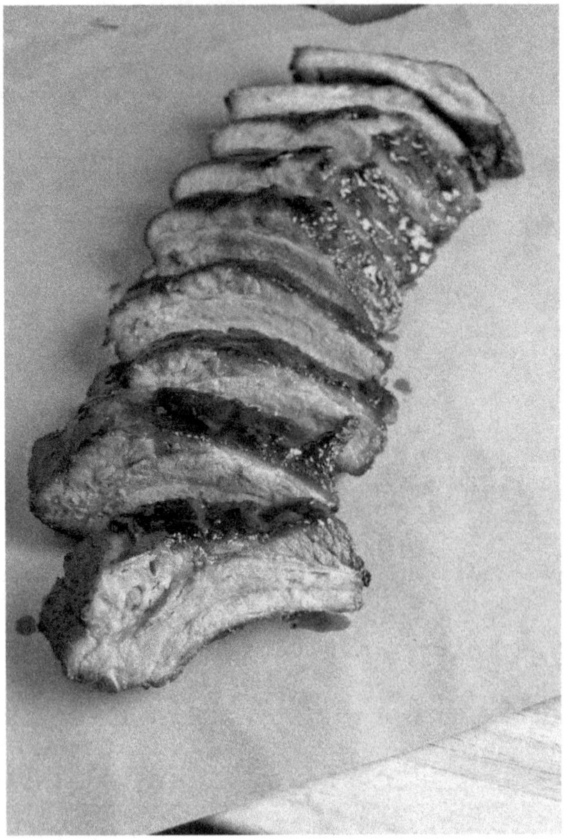

- Course: Dinner
- Cuisine: American
- Total Time: 4 hours 30 minutes
- Preparation Time: 30 minutes
- Cooking Time: 4 hours
- Rest Time: 15 minutes
- Serving Size: 4 servings
- Nutritional Value Per Serving
    - Calories: 302 calories
    - Carbohydrates: 0 g
    - Protein: 22 g

- Fats: 23 g

Equipment Used:

- Electric Smoker

Ingredients:

1. One cut of ribs 1.5 kg
2. Black pepper 1 tsp
3. Paprika 1 tsp
4. Garlic Powder 2 tsp
5. Brown Sugar ¼ cup
6. Salt 1 tsp
7. BBQ sauce ¼ cup

Instructions:

- Prepare the ribs. Trim the extra fat and cut the ribs to easily fit on the Electric Smoker grills.
- Next, prepare the rub for the ribs. In a bowl, mix the pepper, paprika, salt, garlic powder, brown sugar, and salt.
- Rub this mixture on the ribs generously such that all parts of the ribs are rubbed with the herbs.
- Put the ribs in a large zip lock bag and put them in the refrigerator overnight.
- The next day, prepare the electric Smoker with applewood chips. Fill the water tray and turn on the Smoker at 225°F.
- Let the Smoker preheat for 20 minutes.
- Bring out the ribs and arrange them in the smoker racks.

- Place them in the Smoker and let them smoke for 2 hours.
- After 2 hours, take them out, wrap them in aluminum foil, and put them back in the Electric Smoker.
- Let them smoke for a further two hours.
- Take the ribs out and let them rest for 15 minutes.
- After that, unwrap the ribs and serve.

5.12. Smoked Beef Jerky

Commercially prepared beef jerky is commonly available in the market. But there is nothing as flavorful and delicious as homemade beef jerky. In this recipe, we will learn how to prepare beef jerky from scratch.

- Course: Snack
- Cuisine: American
- Total Time: 5 hours
- Preparation Time: 30 minutes

- Cooking Time: 3 hours
- Resting Time: 1 hour
- Serving Size: 5 servings
- Nutritional Value Per Serving
    - Calories: 240 calories
    - Carbohydrates: 1 g
    - Protein: 50 g
    - Fats: 4 g

Equipment Used:

- Electric Smoker

Ingredients:

1. Round beef steak 1.5 kg
2. Honey ¼ cup
3. Soy sauce ¼ cup
4. Worcestershire sauce ¼ cup
5. Brown sugar ¼ cup
6. Garlic Powder 2 tsp
7. Red pepper flakes 1 tbsp
8. Salt 1 tsp
9. Onion Powder 2 tsp

Instructions:

- First, prepare the beef by trimming the extra fat and skin from the meat.
- Next, cut the meat into ¼ inch slices. Make sure that the slices are evenly cut.

- Set the meat aside.
- In a medium-size saucepan, add the honey, soy sauce, Worcestershire sauce, pepper, salt, garlic powder, onion powder, and sugar. Simmer it over the flame until a uniform mixture is formed.
- Let the mixture reach room temperature. Apply the mixture generously on the beef slices and put them in a zip lock bag.
- Pour the remaining sauce into the zip lock bag. Let it in the refrigerator overnight.
- The next day, prepare the electric Smoker with wood chips and water. Turn on the heat at 175° F and preheat for 10 minutes.
- Meanwhile, take out the beef slices and set them on a tray and let them reach room temperature.
- After that, arrange them in an aluminum tray and put them in the Smoker.
- Let the beef smoke for 3 hours.
- Take it out after three hours and rest for about 2 to 3 hours until it becomes dry.
- You can consume it as a snack and store it in an airtight container for up to 2 weeks.

5.13. Striped Bass Recipe

This is a delicious recipe having a mouthwatering flavor. Smoking the fish gives a much better flavor than just grilling. The smokiness makes this dish worth enjoying on a warm summer day. You can have it with a rich tartar sauce, or a little lime juice drizzled on it. If you try this recipe, you are in for a treat.

- Course: Lunch
- Cuisine: American
- Total Time: 3 hours
- Preparation Time: 45 minutes
- Cooking Time: 2 hours
- Serving Size: 6 servings
- Nutritional Value Per Serving
    - Calories: 154 calories
    - Carbohydrates: 0 g
    - Protein: 4 g
    - Fats: 28 g

Equipment Used:

- Electric Smoker

Ingredients:

1. Striped Bass Fillets 1 kg
2. Brown Sugar ¼ cup
3. Water 4 cups

4. Salt ¼ cup
5. Bay leaves 2 leaves.
6. Black pepper 2 tsp
7. Lemon 5 to 6 slices
8. Dry wine ½ cup for brine ½ cup for Smoker
9. Olive oil 3 tsp

Instructions:

- Clean and wash the fish fillets.
- Heat the four cups of water and dissolve salt and sugar in them. Let it come to room temperature.
- When it is at room temperature add, bay leaves, pepper, wine, and lemon slices.
- Put in the fish fillets inside this brine such that they are completely soaked.
- Cover them and leave them overnight.
- The next day prepares the Electric Smoker. Put the alder woodchips in the tray. Fill the water tray half with water and half with white wine.
- Turn on the burner at 180°F.
- Bring out the fish fillets and take them out of the brine and wash them with cold water. Ste them on the counter on a tray lined with paper towels. Let them dry and come to room temperature.
- Meanwhile, coat the smoker grills with olive oil.
- When the fish fillets have reached room temperature, set them on the grills and smoke for two hours.

- The doneness is checked by inserting a thermometer; the internal temperature should be 145◦F.
- Please take out the fish and let it rest for 10 minutes before serving.

5.14. Smoked Cajun Shrimp

Shrimps are a crowd favorite seafood. They are easy to make, and preparation also takes a few minutes. Either you are using fresh shrimps or frozen ones, this recipe works best for both. The only thing is that for frozen shrimps, you will have to defrost them first. This recipe is easy and simple to follow and seldom goes wrong. You will thank us when you have tried this one.

- Course: Appetizer
- Cuisine: American
- Total Time: 1 hour
- Preparation Time: 20 minutes
- Cooking Time: 30 minutes
- Serving Size: 6 servings
- Nutritional Value Per Serving
    - Calories: 92 calories

- Carbohydrates: 2.2.g
- Protein: 4.6 g
- Fats: 7.6 g

Equipment Used:

- Electric Smoker

Ingredients:

1. Jumbo Shrimps 1 kg
2. Salt ¼ cup
3. Dried thyme 2 tbsp
4. Paprika 3 tbsp
5. Cayenne Pepper 2 tsp
6. Onion Powder 2 tbsp
7. Black Pepper 3 tbsp
8. Garlic Powder 2 tbsp
9. Olive Oil 3 tbsp
10. Lemon Juice ¼ cup
11. Fresh Parsley 1 bunch chopped.

Instructions:

- Prepare the shrimps. Take out the shells and devein them. Wash and pat them dry.
- In a bowl prepare the dry rum. Add salt, sugar, cayenne pepper, paprika, garlic powder, thyme, and onion powder. Mix this carefully.
- Next, prepare an aluminum tray by greasing it with olive oil.

- Place the shrimps on the tray in a single layer.
- Apply the dry rum to the shrimps generously.
- Start the electric Smoker at 225°F. Put in the wood chips and water.
- Let it preheat for 20 minutes.
- Meanwhile, pour lemon juice over the shrimps.
- Put the shrimps in the oven for thirty minutes, moving them after every ten minutes.
- Please take out the shrimps after 30 minutes or as soon as they start turning pink.
- This dish can be served warmed or even at room temperature.

5.15. Smoked Scallops

Scallops are juicy and delicious, either grilled or cooked. In this recipe, we have smoked the scallops to give them a rich smokiness. The scallops can be enjoyed with a side of a fresh green salad. This is the ultimate healthy dish to eat for lunch. Do try it out for a different and mouthwatering experience. You will not be disappointed.

- Course: Appetizer
- Cuisine: American
- Total Time: 50 minutes
- Preparation Time: 5 minutes
- Cooking Time: 30 to 40 minutes
- Serving Size: 5 servings
- Nutritional Value Per Serving
    - Calories: 105 calories
    - Carbohydrates: 5 g
    - Protein: 8.7 g
    - Fats: 5.3. g

Equipment used:

- Electric Smoker

Ingredients:

1. Sea Scallops 1 kg
2. Olive oil 3 tbsp
3. Salt 1 tsp
4. Garlic 2 cloves minced.
5. Pepper 1 tsp

Instructions:

- Wash the scallops under cold running water and dry them on a paper towel.
- In a bowl, mix the oil, salt, pepper, and lemon juice.
- Apply the mixture to the scallops.

- Turn on the electric Smoker and prepare it with water and add the wood chips.
- Let it preheat for 10 minutes at 225◦F.
- Meanwhile, lightly grease an aluminum pan and place the scallops on it such that the scallops do not touch each other.
- Put the scallops in the Smoker and smoke for 20 to 30 minutes.
- Check the internal temperature of the scallops.
- Take them out when the temperature reaches 145◦F.
- Let the scallops rest for 10 minutes and then serve with a fresh green salad and a vinaigrette.

100. Smoked Curried Almonds

Almonds are an extremely healthy source of good fats. One enjoys munching them around. This recipe tries a twist on the good old roasted almonds. Let us make snack time fun with these delicious smoked curried almonds. You can keep them for as long as a month and keep enjoying a fistful every day. Heath and taste go hand in hand with this yummy snack.

- Course: Snack
- Cuisine: American
- Total Time: 1 hour 5 minutes
- Preparation Time:5 minutes
- Cooking Time: 1 to 2 hours
- Serving Size: 6 servings
- Nutritional Value Per Serving
    - Calories: 170 calories
    - Carbohydrates: 5 g
    - Protein: 6 g
    - Fats: 15 g

Equipment Used:

- Electric Smoker

Ingredients:

1. Raw Almonds with skins ½ kg
2. Butter 2 tbsp
3. Curry powder 2 tbsp
4. Raw Sugar 2 tbsp
5. 2 tbsp
6. Salt 1 tsp
7. Cayenne Pepper 1 tsp

Instructions:

- Preheat the electric Smoker at 225°F. Fill the water tray half with water and put in the pecan wood chips.
- In a large bowl, mix the butter, salt, sugar, cayenne pepper and curry powder.
- Toss all the almonds in this mixture.
- Prepare an aluminum tray, spread the almonds in the tray as a layer and put it in the Smoker.
- Leave the almonds for one hour and take them out.
- Delicious, curried almonds are ready.
- Let them rest to reach room temperature and enjoy this rich flavorful snack.
- These can be stored in an airtight container for up to 3 months.

101. Smoked Apples with Maple Syrup

If you have a sweet tooth and enjoy fruity desserts, this one is just for you. The naturally citrus flavor of apples is balanced perfectly with the sweetness of maple syrup and raisins. Do try out this recipe; you will not regret it.

- Course: Dessert
- Cuisine: American
- Total Time: 2 hours
- Preparation Time: 30 minutes
- Cooking Time: 1 hour 30 minutes
- Serving Size: 6 servings
- Nutritional Value Per Serving
    - Calories: 224 calories
    - Carbohydrates: 47 g
    - Protein: 1 g
    - Fats: 5 g

Equipment Used:

- Electric Smoker

Ingredients:

1. Apples 6 pieces
2. Maple Syrup ½ cup
3. Raisins ½ cup
4. Cold Butter ¼ cup cut in small cubes.

Instructions:

- Prepare the electric Smoker with water and pecan woodchips. Turn it on at 250°F.
- Take the apples, wash them, and pat dry. Core the apples such that their outer shape is maintained, and a small cavity is formed inside. The apple should still be able to stand without support.
- Fill the lower part of each apple with a small number of raisins, followed by some butter and then the maple syrup.
- Grease an aluminum tray and arrange the apples in the tray.
- Put the apples in the electric Smoker and let them smoke for 1 hour 30 minutes.
- Take them out and let them rest for 10 minutes.
- Serve warm with vanilla ice cream.

102. Smoked Bean Sprouts

Bean sprouts are a great option for a side dish. They can be served with barbecued chicken and are a great source of vitamins and fiber. These are an excellent option for a side dish because they are easy to make and are prepared quickly.

- Course: Side Dish
- Cuisine: American
- Total Time: 1 hour 30 minutes
- Preparation Time: 15 minutes
- Cooking Time: 1 hour
- Serving Size: 6 servings
- Nutritional Value Per Serving
    - Calories: 45 calories
    - Carbohydrates: 8 g
    - Protein: 3 g
    - Fats: 0 g

Equipment Used:

- Electric Smoker

Ingredients:

1. Brussel Sprouts ½ kg
2. Olive Oil 3 tsp

3. Salt 1tsp
4. Pepper ½ tsp

Instructions:

- Wash the Brussel sprouts with cold water and dry them out in a colander.
- Remove the base of the Brussel sprouts and the dried-out parts.
- In a bowl, mix the olive oil, salt, and pepper.
- Apply the mixture to the sprouts and put them in a single layer in an aluminum tray.
- Turn on the electric Smoker at 225°F. Prepare with water and wood chips.
- Let the Smoker preheat for 10 to 15 minutes and then put in the sprouts.
- Let them smoke for 60 minutes.
- Take them out and serve as a side dish with barbeque chicken.

103. Smoked Cauliflower

Cauliflower is super healthy food. It is a rich source of vitamin C and dietary fiber. It contains eighty percent of the recommended amount of Vitamin C required for a day. It fills up your stomach and is slowly digested, thus keeping the stomach filled for a long while.

- Course: Side Dish

- Cuisine: American
- Total Time: 2 hours
- Preparation Time: 5 minutes
- Cooking Time: 2 hours
- Serving Size: 6 servings
- Nutritional Value Per Serving
    - Calories: 129 calories
    - Carbohydrates: 8 g
    - Protein: 3 g
    - Fats: 11 g

Equipment Used:

- Electric Smoker

Ingredients:

1. Cauliflower head 1 big
2. Salt 1 tsp
3. Olive Oil 3 tsp
4. Pepper 1 tsp
5. Balsamic Vinegar 3 tbsp

Instructions:

- Preheat the electric Smoker at 225°F. Fill the water tray and the woodchip tray accordingly.
- Cut the cauliflower head into small florets and wash them with cold water.

- In a bowl, mix the olive oil, balsamic vinegar, salt, and pepper.
- Toss the cauliflower florets in the bowl.
- In an aluminum tray, layer the cauliflower florets and put them in the Smoker.
- Smoke for 2 hours, turning the florets once midway.
- Take out after two hours and serve as a side dish.

5.20. Smoked Cherry Tomatoes

Smoked cherry tomatoes are not a dish in themselves but can form a base for other dishes like salads and pasta. This recipe is included here because smoked cherry tomatoes add flavor and richness to the foods they are mixed with. To add a rich smoky flavor to pasta, you can add cherry tomatoes. Adding smoked cherry tomatoes to a salad hive is the required kick to the otherwise boring salad. Smoked cherry tomatoes are uses as a side dish in Middle Eastern food commonly.

- Course: Side Dish
- Cuisine: American

- Total Time: 1 hour 5 minutes
- Preparation Time: 5 minutes
- Cooking Time: 1 hour
- Serving Size: 4 servings
- Nutritional Value Per Serving
  - Calories: 25 calories
  - Carbohydrates: 3.6 g
  - Protein: 1.1 g
  - Fats: 0.5 g

Equipment Used:

- Electric Smoker

Ingredients:

1. Cherry Tomatoes 300g

Instructions:

- Preheat the electric Smoker to 225◦F. Fill half of the water tray of the Smoker and fill in the wood chips.
- Wash the cherry tomatoes with cold water and spread them on a paper towel.
- Arrange the cherry tomatoes in the aluminum tray and put them in the Smoker.
- Leave the tomatoes for 60 minutes and then take them out.
- You will observe that the cherry tomatoes have burst open, and the juices are oozing out.

- Do not waste the juices; these juices also give off a smokey and delicious taste to salads and pasta.

5.21. Sweet and Spicy Chicken Wings

Chicken wings are another crowd favorite. This recipe used a lot of spices and cut the overpowering spicy flavor; sugar is used. The sugar gives a sweet taste and a crispy finish with its caramelization. This is a perfect dish if you are planning to host a barbecue party.

- Course: Lunch
- Cuisine: American
- Total Time: 1 hour 50 minutes
- Preparation Time:20 minutes
- Cooking Time: 1 hour 30 minutes
- Serving Size: 4 servings
- Nutritional Value Per Serving
    - Calories: 356 calories
    - Carbohydrates: 23.9 g
    - Protein: 15.6 g
    - Fats: 22.7 g

Equipment Used:

- Electric Smoker

Ingredients:

1. Chicken wings 2.5 kg
2. Salt 2 tsp
3. Pepper 1 tsp
4. Onion Powder 1 tsp
5. Garlic Powder 1tsp
6. Paprika ¼ cup
7. Cayenne Pepper 1 tsp
8. Brown Sugar ½ cup

Instructions:

- Wash the chicken wings with cold water and trim them.
- If you wish, you can break the wings in half or keep them full. Depends on your preference.
- Next, mix the paprika, salt, pepper, onion powder, garlic powder, sugar, and cayenne pepper in a big mixing bowl.
- Toss the chicken wings into this spice rub. Use your hands to coat the chicken wings with the spice rub.
- Turn on the electric Smoker at 250°F. Put water in the water tray and fill the wood chip tray with wood chips.
- Let the Smoker preheat for 15 minutes.
- Meanwhile, take out the grill from the Smoker and arrange the wings on the grill.

- Put in the wings in the Smoker and smoke for 2 hours. Check the internal temperature of the chicken should be 165◦F.
- Take out the chicken wings and serve them hot.

5.22. Herbal Chicken Wings

This is a delicious recipe of chicken wings that has a strong flavor of herbs and spices. This recipe is inspired by French cuisine. Make this recipe to enjoy the Parisian feel in the comfort of your own house.

- Course: Lunch
- Cuisine: American
- Total Time: 3 hours 20 minutes

- Preparation Time: 10 minutes
- Cooking Time:
- Serving Size: 4 servings
- Nutritional Value Per Serving
    - Calories: 220 calories
    - Carbohydrates: 0 g
    - Protein: 18 g
    - Fats: 16 g

Equipment Used:

- Electric Smoker

Ingredients:

1. Chicken Wings 2.5 kg
2. Olive oil ½ cup
3. Garlic 2 cloves minced.
4. Rosemary Leaves 2 tbsp
5. Fresh basil leaves 2 tbsp.
6. Lemon Juice 2 tbsp
7. Salt 1 ½ tsp
8. Pepper 1tsp
9. Oregano 2 tbsp

Instructions:

- Prepare the chicken wings by trimming them. Wash the wings under cold running water.

- It is your choice to break the wings into half or use them as it is.
- In a large mixing bowl, add all ingredients and herbs and make a smooth mixture.
- Save half and toss the chicken wings in the other half.
- Use your hands to toss the wings in the mixture so that it is evenly applied.
- Preheat the electric Smoker at 250◦F and prepare it with water and wood chips.
- Arrange the wings on the smoker racks and smoke them for two hours.
- The doneness is determined by achieving a 165◦F temperature internally.
- Take out the wings and serve them hot.

5.23. Smoked Redfish

In this fish, we are using a dry brine technique. This is an easy and quick recipe; however, it requires the fish to marinate overnight. If you are planning to call guests over, you can prepare the fish fillets in advance.

- Course: Lunch
- Cuisine: American
- Total Time: 2 hours 10 minutes

- Preparation Time: 10 minutes
- Cooking Time: 2 hours
- Serving Size: 6 servings
- Nutritional Value Per Serving
    - Calories: 160 calories
    - Carbohydrates: 2 g
    - Protein: 18 g
    - Fats: 4 g

Equipment Used:

- Electric Smoker

Ingredients:

1. 2 redfish fillets with skin 600g
2. Salt half cup
3. Black pepper 1tsp
4. Lemon Zest 1 tsp
5. Garlic powder 1tsp
6. Lemon 2or 4 slices

Instructions:

- Wash the fish fillets with cold running water.
- Next, prepare a rub by mixing all the ingredients and spices.
- Apply the rub on the fish fillets generously. Wrap the fish fillets in cling film and refrigerate them overnight.
- The next day take out the fish fillets and bring them to room temperature.

- Prepare the electric Smoker with wood chips and water. Turn it on at 170◦F.
- When the fillets are at room temperature, wash them and pat them dry.
- Put them in the Smoker for two hours.
- After two hours, check the internal temperature. It should be 140◦F.
- Let the fillets rest for 30 minutes before serving.

5.24. Smoked Dory

This fish is easy to cook and quickly prepared. We will use the dry rub method to prepare the dory fish fillets. This turns out to be a delicious recipe and is a crowd favorite.

- Course: Dinner
- Cuisine: American
- Total Time: 1 hour 15 minutes
- Preparation Time: 15 minutes
- Cooking Time: 1 hour
- Serving Size: 4 servings
- Nutritional Value Per Serving

- Calories: 175 calories
- Carbohydrates: 2 g
- Protein: 22 g
- Fats: 8 g

Equipment Used:

- Electric Smoker

Ingredients:

1. 4 fillets of dory fish 800g
2. Onion Powder
3. Salt half cup
4. Black pepper 2tsp
5. Ginger powder 1 tsp
6. Garlic powder 1tsp
7. Coriander for garnish
8. Lemon slices for garnish

Instructions:

- Wash the fish fillets with cold running water.
- Next, prepare a rub by mixing all the ingredients and spices.
- Apply the rub on the fish fillets generously. Wrap the fish fillets in cling film and refrigerate them overnight.
- The next day take out the fish fillets and bring them to room temperature.
- Prepare the electric Smoker with wood chips and water. Turn it on at 220°F.
- When the fillets are at room temperature, wash them and pat them dry.

- Could you put them in the Smoker for two hours?
- After one hour, check the internal temperature. It should be 160◦F.
- Let the fillets rest for 30 minutes before serving.
- Garnish the fish fillets with coriander and lemon slices for serving.

5.25. Herbal Smoked Salmon

Salmon is one fish variety that is consumed very often among people. The reason for this is that it is an excellent source of protein, and it cooks easily. Smoked salmon is something that you can enjoy at family dinners and other gatherings. You can never go wrong with smoked salmon.

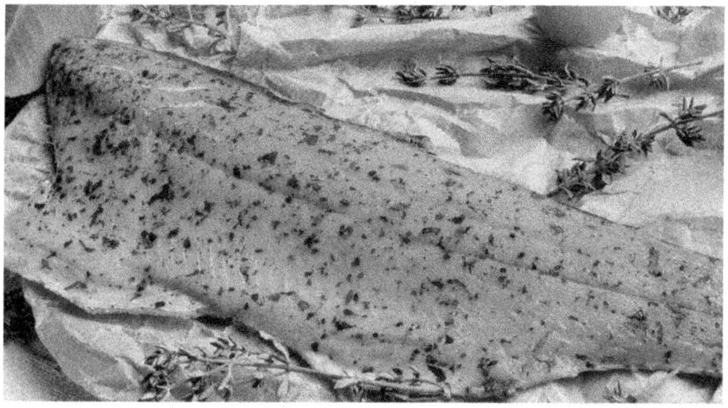

- Course: Dinner
- Cuisine: American
- Total Time: 4 hours 30 minutes
- Preparation Time: 30 minutes
- Cooking Time: 4 hours
- Serving Size: 4 servings
- Nutritional Value Per Serving
    - Calories: 210 calories
    - Carbohydrates: o g

- Protein: 22.3. g
- Fats: 12.3 g

Equipment Used:

- Electric Smoker

Ingredients:

1. Salmon fillets 750 g
2. Salt ¼ cup
3. Sugar ¼ cup
4. Water ½ cup
5. Black Pepper 2 tbsp
6. Lemon 2 slices
7. Fresh dill chopped 1 bunch.

Instructions:

- Prepare the marinade for the fish. In a flat dish, pour water, salt, sugar, and pepper. Mix them well.
- Soak the fish fillets in the marinade and cover them with dill and lemon slices.
- Wrap the fillets in cling wrap and refrigerate overnight.
- The next day, prepare the Electric Smoker. Put the wood chips and water in the water tray.
- Turn on the electric Smoker at 180°F. Put the fish fillets on the grill and smoke for four hours.

- In this recipe, we are smoking the fish at a lower temperature for a longer time. If you have a time constraint, you can use a higher temperature for a shorter period.
- Check the doneness of the fish by inserting the thermometer. The internal temperature must be 130°F.
- Take out the fish and let it rest for 30 minutes before serving.

5.26. Smoked Stuffed Mushroom

These stuffed mushrooms can be served by themselves and can be served as a side dish as well. Try this recipe, and you will not be disappointed.

- Course: Side Dish
- Cuisine: American
- Total Time: 1 hour 15 minutes
- Preparation Time: 20 minutes
- Cooking Time: 55 minutes
- Serving Size: 6 servings
- Nutritional Value Per Serving
    - Calories: 320 calories
    - Carbohydrates: 22 g

- Protein: 8 g
- Fats: 7 g

Equipment Used:

- Electric Smoker

Ingredients:

1. Button Mushrooms with stem 24 mushroom
2. Onion 1 minced
3. Garlic 2 cloves minced.
4. Salt ½ tsp
5. Black Pepper 1 tsp
6. Breadcrumbs ¾ cup
7. Parmesan cheese ¾ cup
8. Olive Oil 1/3 cup
9. Parsley ¼ cup

Instructions:

- Preheat the electric Smoker at 250°F. Put the wood chips in the tray and water in the water tray.
- In a saucepan, put in some olive oil and sauté the onion and garlic in it.
- In another mixing bowl, mix the breadcrumbs, cheese and salt and black pepper.
- Cut the stems of the mushrooms and chop them. Add the chopped stems to the saucepan with the onion and garlic and cook for one minute.
- Set an aluminum tray and set the mushroom heads up-side-down in a layer.

- Mix the onion, garlic, and mushrooms into the cheese mixture.
- Put a spoonful of mixture on the mushroom heads.
- Put the mushrooms in the Smoker and smoke for 45 minutes.
- Take out the mushrooms and let them rest for 20 minutes before serving.

5.27. Smoked Chicken Breast

This is a simple recipe and can never go wrong. Easy to make and delicious to taste. You can prepare this overnight and smoke it the next day. Family and friends will enjoy it alike.

- Course: Dinner
- Cuisine: American
- Total Time: 5 hours
- Preparation Time: 20 minutes

- Cooking Time: 4 hours 30 minutes
- Serving Size: 4 servings
- Nutritional Value Per Serving
    - Calories: 280 calories
    - Carbohydrates: 2 g
    - Protein: 23 g
    - Fats: 4 g

Equipment Used:

- Electric Smoker

Ingredients:

1. 4 chicken breast pieces 1 kg
2. Black pepper 2 tsp
3. Salt 2 tsp
4. Lemon Juice 4 tbsp
5. Paprika 2 tbsp

Instructions:

- Wash the chicken breast pieces. It is your choice to remove the skin or keep it.
- Pat the chicken dry.
- In a flat dish, mix the salt, pepper, paprika and lemon juice.
- Apply the mixture generously on the chicken and wrap the pieces with cling wrap and leave it in the refrigerator overnight.

- The next day, prepare the electric Smoker with the wood chips and water. Preheat the Smoker at 180◦F.
- Bring the chicken fillets at room temperature and wash them under cold running water.
- Pat the chicken dries with paper towels and arrange them on the racks of the Smoker.
- Smoke the chicken for about 4 hours and 30 minutes.
- Check the temperature of the chicken. It will be done when the internal temperature reaches 165◦F.
- Take out the chicken and let it rest for 30 minutes before serving.
- Serve with your choice of side dishes.

Introduction

The hottest trend in the BBQ and grilling community have been pellet grills. Since technology has not really improved much in the industry in the last three decades or so, individuals are enthusiastic about the amazing functionality and comfort that pellet grills are bringing to the sector. However, it's crucial to learn how they function in order to fully appreciate what they have to deliver. So, if you're new to grilling or smoking pellets and you're thinking about how pellet grills operate, then you've come to the right place.

Barbecuing is the oldest form of cooking worldwide. Low-and-slow smoking and cooking over indirect heat is the standard concept of barbecuing. There is little question regarding the findings obtained from barbecuing utilizing haze, indirect fire, sauces, rubs, and natural meat juices. Among grilling and barbecuing, there is a big distinction, but many people are ignorant because they use all words loosely.

Smoker-grills with wood pellets is ideal units for barbecuing.

In this book, you will get to know each and everything you need to learn about the know-how of a Wood Pellet Smoker Grill.

This book provides you with various tips and tricks that you need to know in order to enjoy the process of barbequing and making it a deliciously funny activity.

Also, various basic recipes are provided for you to start with your grilling with ease in the comfort of your home.

Chapter 1- Wood Pellet Smoker Grills

1.1 What is a Pellet Smoker Grill?

A barbecue pit using compressed hardwood sawdust such as apple, plum, hickory, pine, oak, mesquite, and other wood pellets to roast, grill, smoke and bake is the clinical concept of a wood pellet smoker-grill. The smoker-grill wood pellet provides you with taste profiles and moisture that can only be obtained through hardwood cooking. Grill temperatures on certain versions vary from 150 °F to well over 600 °F, depending on the maker and platform.

Wood pellet smoker-grills are succulent, cosy and clean, unparalleled by gas grills and charcoal. The smoke composition is milder than you may be accustomed to from other cigarettes. They produce the flexibility and advantages of a convection oven due to their architecture. Smoker-grills with wood pellets is safe and easy to work.

In short outdoor cookers that incorporate components from smokers, kitchen ovens, charcoal smokers, and gas grills are pellet grills. They use 100% of natural hardwood pellets, the fuel supply that enables direct or indirect heat to be generated by Pellet Grills.

Fueled by wood pellets, utilizing an electronic control panel, they will smoke and grill and bake to automatically feed fuel pellets to the flames, regulate the ventilation of the grill, and maintain constant cooking temperatures.

1.2 Working of a Pellet Smoker Grill

Wood pellets are placed into a hopper-called storage container. An auger that is operated by electricity then feeds the pellets into a cooking chamber. The wood pellets ignite by combustion, warming the cooking chamber. After that, the air is pulled in by intake fans. Across the boiling area, flame and smoke are then emitted.

Rather like an oven, pellet grills provide you digitally or with a knob with reliable temperature regulation, typically varying from 180 ° F to 500 ° F. So, "low and slow" or searing hot both can be cooked by you.

In order to check the core temperature of the beef, most pellet grills do have a meat probe that can link with the control board. There is a proprietary Sear Zone plate for grills that requires implicit or explicit heat and eight separate cooking methods.

1.3 Basic Components of a Wood Pellet Smoker

The following provided are the basic components of a wood pellet smoker grill: -

1. Hopper

This is where they store the wood pellets. Be sure you hold a good quantity of pellets based on the cook's range, the cook's temperature, and the capability of the hopper.

2. Firepot

This is where the fire and burn the wood pellets that ignite the barbecue. For the pellet shaft, which holds the auger, the wide hole in the firepot is; the bottom center gap below it is for the igniter tube, and the other holes are for the ventilation of the fan. After a few cooks, it is a good idea to empty or vacuum out the ashes in order to enable the igniter to function more effectively.

3. Auger

The pellets are then loaded via the auger, the feed system that provides the fire pot with the pellets.

4. Fan

As it ensures a constant and/or steady airflow, the fan is very critical, maintaining the pellets trying to burn in the firepot and culminating in cooking convection.

5. Igniter Rod

The wood pellets are ignited in the firepot by this rod. The ignitor rod and the pellet feed tube that is required by the auger to supply pellets to the firepot can be seen with the firepot away.

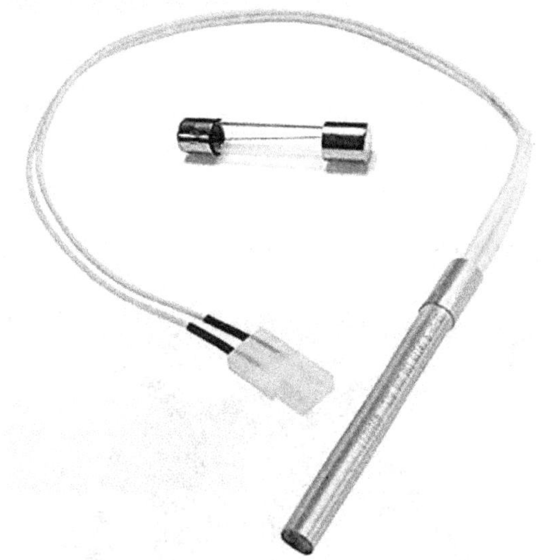

6. Hear Deflector

A specially crafted plate covering the firepot is the heat deflector. The goal is to absorb the heat and distribute it uniformly under the grease/drip plate, converting the wood pellet smoker-grill into a wood-fired convection oven effectively.

7. Resistive Temperature Detector (RTD) / Thermocouple

The thermal sensor that supplies the input loop to the controller is the RTD or thermocouple. For better heat readings, deep clean the thermocouple regularly.

8. Flame Zone Pan

For clear, high-temperature grilling, it is used in tandem with searing grates and attachments for the griddle.

9. Drip Pan

In indirect frying, smoking, baking and roasting, the oiled pan is used. It routes the grease generated to the grease bucket during cooking. It is recommended to scrape off an appropriate caked-on residue from cooks. Also, substitute the foil per few cooks if utilizing foil.

10. Grease Bucket

Runoff fat and oil from cooking activities are extracted from the grease bucket. Accumulation of grease relies on how often you want to cut from beef and poultry fat caps and extra fat. Lining the foil grease bowl tends you clear up.

11. Controller

To preserve the set-point temperature, the controller, which normally comes in several types, regulates the air and pellet movement.

1.4 Using your Wood Pellet Smoker Grill

1. Assembly

If a nearby distributor assembles your product for you or you order your unit from a big box retailer, you will need to install your wood pellet smoker-grill. Whether you order the product directly from the vendor or via an online distributor, the unit would also be shipped on a pallet by a ground carrier. But don't dread; assembly isn't as rough as it seems or as complicated as you would imagine.

Only set out all of the bits, and yes, before you begin assembly, make sure you read the directions. Tech help and assistance are just a phone call away, and several suppliers have excellent customer care.

You'll find the design and directions will help you to create your smoker-grill wood pellet easily in an hour or less. In most units, the foundation and legs are often mounted. You will have your device full of wood pellets and ready for the initial burn-in in no time. Be sure you have someone to support you if and where the directions ask for two persons. By choosing to do things yourself, do not harm yourself.

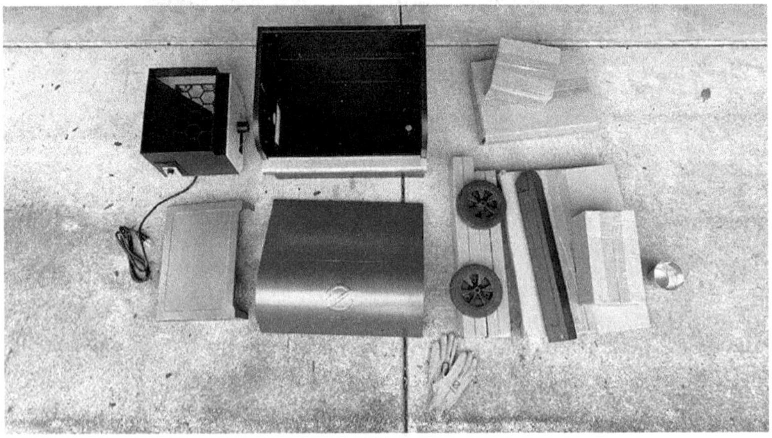

2. Ignition

Wood pellet smoker-grills require standard household 120 VAC or 12 VDC outlets. For powering the ignition and service, wood pellet smoker-grills require regular household 120 VAC or 12 VDC outlets. For, e.g., certain devices, such as the Davy Crockett tailgate device from Green Mountain Grills, are built to use 12 VDC from a car battery or a deep-cycle battery. They also have a 120 VAC AC/DC converter for usage. The power requirements are actually very limited for wood pellet smoker-grills and are used for four items: fan, auger, controller and igniter rod.

Smoker-grills with wood pellets are very safe and easy to work. Inside the fire pot, the fire/flames are limited and completely protected by the oil pan, which gives indirect cooking and avoids flare-ups. Typically, based on the maker, one of two factors can arise when you turn on your device. Your pit either goes through a particular power-up series, or a typical scenario follows it.

The controller is flipped on, the igniter rod is triggered (it will glow red hot), the auger feeds a certain volume of pellets into the firepot, and the fan feeds air into the firepot through numerous tiny holes to start and sustain the fire. The igniter rod is either switched off after a fixed period (4 minutes or longer) or when the pit exceeds a set temperature, depending on your controller. To stop flame-outs, PID controllers can switch the igniter rod back on when the temperature falls below a fixed temperature.

3. Initial Burn-In

To burn out all oils and chemicals used in the processing phase, the burn-in technique is used.

With hardwood barbecue-grade wood pellets, fill the hopper. Because the transmission of the first pellets to the firepot can take ten or more minutes for the auger, put half a handful of pellets in the firepot. Attach the device into a 120 VAC electrical socket with grounding. Just turn on your grill. Place temperature between 350 ° F and 450 ° F if you have a digital controller, and allow the grill to operate at temperature for 30 to 60 minutes (check your owner's manual for precise temperature settings and time). Convert the temperature setting to strong if your grill has an LMH controller.

4. Testing for Hot Spots on Your Wood Pellet Smoker-Grill

Not all wood pellet smoker-grills are identical, but I promise that you will be able to smoke and prepare some of the best food your family and friends will ever experience by knowing about your barbecue! To have a working knowledge of the barbecue, it just takes a few cooks to train.

You'll want to monitor the temperature of the grill surface for uniform heat and hotspots. The biscuit test is one simple way to do this.

In the corners, front, back, and middle of the barbecue pick up a box of refrigerator biscuits and position them. As per the instructions on the box, cook the biscuits. You can discover where the hotter and colder places are in your device with this exercise.

Place your food and prepare it according to the data you've gained.

The use of a remote temperature probe to measure the temperatures at the same positions as the biscuit test is needed for a more technical process. At each biscuit spot, put a remote temperature probe, check the temperature, contrast it to the fixed point on your controller and, if any, record the temperature variations. No matter how nice your grill controller is, regardless of the position of the RTD/thermocouple, you'll notice discrepancies. To attain the temperatures you like, just change your grill's fixed temperatures accordingly.

5. Cleaning Your Wood Pellet Smoker-Grill

It is highly recommended that you keep your smoker-grill with wood pellets as clean as possible. It only takes a couple of minutes to keep the pit clean before you cook. Cleanliness ensures that your cooks are always penetrated with fresh and clean smoke. For the best results, after every hard cook or after every two to four short cooks, replace the foil on the grease drop pan. If you choose not to use foil, then make sure that the caked residue is often scraped off from your drip pan. There is nothing other than the gases burning off at elevated temperatures from rancid old grease. Using a barbecue wire brush to scrub and hold them clean after each cooker, when the grill grates are still hot. Wipe down both sides of the grates using paper towels. When handling the grates and cleaning your pit, I strongly suggest you wear disposable rubber gloves.

Once your pit fully cools down, remove the drip pan and regularly remove any ash from the firepot and the body of the pit using a shop vacuum cleaner. Although smoker-grills with wood pellets are incredibly effective, you will still accumulate some ash.

Large quantities of ash in the firepot will decrease the unit's efficiency and might not cause the igniter rod to ignite pellets properly at star-tup. During a roast, an ash accumulation in the body of the pit has a chance to be blown around and collected on the beef.

Chapter 2-Tricks and Techniques

2.1 Quality Meat and Seasonings

For excellent and personalized cuts of meats, sausages and poultry, and as well as wonderful rubs, seasonings, and barbecue sauces, don't forget your friendly neighbourhood butcher shop.

Low-and-slow cooking, grilling, smoking, frying, roasting, etc., are always worth the seasoning.

It is strongly suggested that you go out and visit the nearest butcher shops and meat markets to see if you can even locate the jewel in the rough that will create an excellent crowd of your next chef.

FTC-In order to redistribute the juices into the product, this significant acronym stands for "Foil-Towel-Cooler" and is a popular process used for retaining and/or resting cooked meats, such as pork butts, turkey and brisket. It provides a final product that is juicy and tender. For example, to accomplish these effects, pit masters, professionals, caterers, and restaurants utilize industrial units such as a Cambro. The FTC is lovingly referred to as the Cambro of the unfortunate guy.

To hold the juices contained, double-wrap the cooked meat in heavy-duty aluminium foil. Before you put it in a cooler, cover the foiled meat in a wide towel. Minimize air room if needed by covering the majority of the cooler with towels to help prevent the heat from dissipating. Depending on the meat and/or the period available before serving, FTC pork butts and briskets are processed in a locked cooler for a minimum of 2 hours and up to 4 to 6 hours. When processing meat, take care, since it may always be too hot to handle even after resting for hours.

2.2 USDA Minimum Internal Temperatures

As determined with an automated food thermometer, cook all food at these required internal temperatures before extracting it from the heat source. For purposes of personal choice, you can choose to cook at higher temperatures.

1. **Indirect and Direct Grill Setup**

Both smoker-grills with wood pellets are built mainly for indirect cooking. To cook more slowly and uniformly, indirect cooking utilizes deflected fire. The heat deflector is a stainless-steel plate that sits above the fire pot, as described before. It collects the heat from the fire and radiates it out like a convection oven does, ensuring that the heat is spread around it, giving a cook that is more uniform. Direct cooking uses direct, high heat to cook, much as the name suggests. It's a quicker time to cook, which doesn't make for many infusions of smoke, but it does give you the iconic grill marks. More producers are now starting to provide the versatility of a direct cooking setup, and a limited number have a built-in hybrid design that both offers indirect and direct cooking power without needing to alter any configuration.

- **Indirect Setup**

You'll be using an indirect rig for several wood pellet smoker-grill recipes. Per your manufacturer's user manual, mount your grease pan. In order for the grease fat to fall out, the Grease pan is built to slant in the path of the grease bucket. Otherwise, at higher temperatures, the grease would collect on the pan, which might become a flare-up safety problem.

- **Direct Setup**

You will need to swap your indirect pan with a direct pan because your machine has built-in direct cooking capabilities. To customize it for direct cooking, you can need to detach one or more cover plates in certain units or slip the top part of a combination pan. To close or expose the gaps, you slip the cover in one direction or the other. Shuttered holes are for indirect cooking, whereas direct cooking is for open holes. Searing gratings are not obligatory. They can have greater results when grilling and cooking directly since they are built to sear and sizzle foods easier by focusing the fire.

2. Ingredients

Feel free to replace, delete, and incorporate some ingredients dependent on your tastes, taste buds, and ingredients on hand, depending on how relaxed you are in the kitchen or with the grill. Strict adherence to the list of ingredients can deliver impressive results, but do not be afraid to tweak it here and there.

3. Prepping for the Grill

Before taking the food to the barbecue, the prep portion is all the preparation you do. Planning ahead is the number one goal in the prep period. Offer yourself plenty of time, read the recipe, and examine every move or process in which you can have concerns. To allow the seasonings, rubs, marinades and brines to do their magic, recipes can call for refrigeration overnight or for hours after making preparations. Before beginning your preparation, gather all required ingredients and cooking equipment. Before starting, make sure the proteins are safely thawed in the refrigerator if you do not use fresh beef, poultry, or seafood. Be vigilant to have good sanitary facilities, above all.

There may be occasions when the processes of planning and guidance can occur concurrently. You may opt to preheat before finishing the cooking, based on the length of time your wood pellet smoker-grill needs to preheat, much as in a conventional indoor oven.

4. On the Wood Pellet Smoker Grill

Unless otherwise stated, it is strongly recommended to start with a complete pellet hopper and a clean wood pellet smoker-grill configured for indirect fire. If required, prior to putting the meat on the plate, insert the grill meat probe(s) or remote meat probe(s) into the thickest part of the protein. Bear in mind that each smoker grill for wood pellets is different, and so the time to create various recipes may vary accordingly. Depend on internal temperatures at all times. Just to find out that it's undercooked, you won't believe how scrumptious a piece of meat might look.

You can soon discover when you grow confident with your wood pellet smoker-grill that cooking directions can be adjustable as long as the correct internal temperature is met by your finished product.

2.3 General Information and Tips

1. Preheating

According to factory start-up procedures, times for heating up your wood pellet smoker-grill can differ. The trick is to run a few experiments to grasp your barbecue.

2. Thawing Food

Always thaw food in the refrigerator to be healthy to avoid illness; immerse it in freezing water, adjust the water every 30 minutes and ensure that the food remains submerged; or use the freezer to defrost the food. On the countertop, do not thaw the frozen food.

3. Internal Temperature

Often use a wireless instant-read thermometer such as a Thermapen or an analogous device to cook at internal temperatures. Before putting the protein on the grill, probe thermometers should be inserted and put in the thickest section of the beef, not reaching the bone.

4. Tenting

Until slicing or eating, many recipes ask for resting the meat under a foil tent. Tenting is a simple process.

In the middle, fold sheets of aluminium foil, fan it opens into a tent form and position it loosely over the food. Instead of placing them on the serving tray, tenting tends to preserve heat as the food redistributes the natural juices. By tenting, crispy skin texture on poultry and crisp on meats may be affected.

5. The Stall

A natural part of the cooking process is the stall, also known as the plateau or zone. Large cuts of meat reach a point when cooked at low temperatures, where the core temperature stops rising for a period of time. After the collagen melts, most cuts of meat tenderize, and the fibres begin to separate. The stall will experience every big chunk of meat, such as a pork butt (shoulder) or beef brisket. It can last minutes or as long as three hours and normally occurs from 155 ° F to 170 ° F at internal meat temperatures. It's not a question of whether, but when, the stall is going to happen. In your wood pellet smoker-grill, you may be tempted to turn the heat up, but practice patience; just ride it out so as not to affect the meat being cooked.

6. The Texas Crutch

A technique is commonly known as the "Texas crutch" will decrease your cooking time and bypass the stall for those who cannot wait out the stall. The most preferred version of the Texas crutch is to consider removing the meat from the stall before it reaches its full size. When the internal temperature reaches 160 °F, remove the meat, then double wrap it in heavy-duty aluminium foil, ensuring that any meat probes are inserted into the meat. Wrap the foil around the probe until it attains your desired internal temperature, and return the meat to the grill.

7. Carving Meat

Always carve meat across the grain, not with it, to get the most tender outcomes. Searching for the simultaneous lines running down the meat identifies the direction that the grain is running. Slice the muscle fibre lines perpendicular to them.

8. Protect your Skin

While handling raw meat and spicy peppers like jalapeños, wear food-grade latex-free nitric gloves.

9. Keep your Prep Surface Clean

It is highly recommended that plastic food wrap and/or heavy-duty aluminium foil line your prep area. When dealing with raw meat, this simplifies clean-up and is also more hygienic.

10. Curing Salt

Curing salt contains salt and nitrite, which is used in some low-and-slow recipes and should not be used to season food at the table or during the cooking process. Significant quantities can be lethal, but when curing meat, it is harmless in small quantities.

11. Smoke Issues

The higher the temperature, the lower smoke is produced by a wood pellet smoker-grill. No noticeable smoke above 300°F will be produced by most units. Therefore, when a recipe initially calls for extremely high temperatures, use any pellets of your choice, as the pellets will not influence the flavour.

2.4 Simple tricks for beginners

1. Allow yourself some time to get acquainted with your new grill/smoker

Allow yourself time to familiarize yourself with your new grill/smoker. We know you're going to be anxious to give it a try, but don't be overly ambitious. Start with chicken, salmon steaks or fillets, pork loin tenderloin, Cornish hens, blade steaks, or other fairly affordable cuts that can be completed in 2 hours or less, instead of a whole brisket that might take 15 hours or more, or a budget-busting prime rib roast.

2. Don't let your meat come to room temperature before cooking

Whichever meat you select, put it straight from the refrigerator on the preheated grill/smoker. Do not allow it to reach room temperature before cooking, as many recipes suggest.

3. Take advantage of your pellet grill's searing capabilities

Many pellet grills feature searing capabilities, which means that temperatures above 500 °C can be reached. Again, for information on your particular model, check your owner's manual.

4. Use the reverse sear method

Don't think about smoking the meat at a lower temperature and then finishing it at a high temperature. This two-step approach is particularly useful for smoking crisp (not rubbery) skin chicken, or the "reverse sear technique" often used for thicker steaks or prime ribs.

5. Use your pellet grill just like an oven

Just like an oven, your smoker/pellet grill can be used, capable of baking, roasting, braising, etc. But the inclusion of wood smoke gives much more fascinating flavours to food.

6. Experiment with pellet flavours

Experiment with the flavours of pellets. Certain pellet labels are somewhat subtle.

7. Position your grill at least 6 feet away from your home

At least six feet from any buildings, overhangs, bushes, etc., place your barbecue.

8. Always store pellets in a dry place

Pellets can always be kept in a dry spot. Otherwise, it'll transform to sawdust, and if it's an augur, to anything like a stone!

9. Use the upper rack of your grill for cooking something that's prone to drying out

Convection and radiant heat are also generated by your pellet grill. Place them on the upper rack to shield them from the heat radiating from the bottom while you are frying anything that is vulnerable to drying out, such as thin fish fillets or chicken breasts. You can balance a wire rack on fire bricks or buy after-market racks if your machine doesn't come with an upper rack. To produce moisture, you may also place a pan of water or other liquid on the grill grate.

10. Season your new pellet grill

Season your new pellet grill according to directions from the manufacturer. This burns off the production process of any residual oils.

11. Identify any hot spots—most grills have them

As directed by the owner's manual, preheat your grill to medium-high, then lay slices of cheap white bread shoulder to shoulder across the grater. Watch carefully, then after a couple of minutes, flip. Take a photo of the findings. The darkest bread will show where the temperature could be warmer

12. Invest in a good meat thermometer

At grill level, a laser-type thermometer will give you a more precise temperature reading than an integrated dome thermometer. Determine your grill model's temperature range from lowest to highest.

13. Use lower temperatures to generate more smoke

At lower temperatures, especially in the "low and slow" range between 225 and 275, you will generate more smoke.

14. Never allow the pellets in the pellet hopper to run out

Never allow it to run out of the pellets in the pellet hopper. If this occurs, before relighting the barbecue, check the owner's manual. To reassure yourself to top off the pellets, set a timer if you have to.

15. Invest in a smoking tube to supplement the smoke generated by your grill

If you want to complement your pellet grill with the smoke produced, or even cold smoke, engage in a smoking tube.

16. Clean your grill frequently

To prevent the build-up of ash or oil, clean your grill regularly. Much like a sharp-bladed spatula or putty knife, a shop-type vacuum is a must. Don't neglect to sweep the exhaust or chimney.

17. Use heavy-duty foil for easier clean-up

To protect the oil tray and to line the grease bucket, use high-duty foil. (Also, hollow containers may be used as bucket liners, such as coffee or tomato cans.)

18. **Remove the grease bucket after each cook**

Take the grease bucket off the side of the grill after each cooker and hide it in a secure position to keep it out of the hands of pets, coyotes or other hungry creatures.

19. Smoke vegetables and side dishes on your new grill

Using the new grill to smoke or roast vegetables or side dishes.

Chapter 3-Appetizers Recipes

3.1 Atomic Buffalo Turds

Ready in about 2 hours and 50 minutes | Servings-6 to 10 | Difficulty-Hard

Ingredients

- 3⁄4 cup of shredded Monterey Jack and cheddar cheese blend
- Half teaspoon of red pepper flakes
- Eight ounces of regular cream cheese
- Ten medium jalapeño peppers
- One teaspoon of garlic powder
- Ten thinly sliced bacon strips, cut in half
- One teaspoon of smoked paprika
- Twenty Little Smokies sausages
- Half teaspoon of cayenne pepper

Instructions

1. Firstly, if you use your food service gloves, we need to ready the grill for that. Clean the jalapeño peppers and slice them lengthwise. Carefully extract the seeds and veins using a spoon or paring knife, and dispose of them. On a vegetable grilling tray, put the jalapeños and set them aside.

2. Mix the cream cheese, shredded cheese, paprika, cayenne pepper, garlic powder, and red pepper flakes in a small cup, if using, until they are thoroughly absorbed.

3. With the cream cheese mixture, cover the hollowed jalapeño pepper pieces.

4. On top of each half of the packed jalapeño pepper, put a Little Smokies sausage.

5. Wrap each half of the jalapeño pepper with half a slice of thin bacon.

6. To secure the bacon to the sausage, use a toothpick, making sure not to pierce the pepper. On a grilling tray or skillet, position the ABTs.

7. For indirect cooking, set up your wood pellet smoker-grill and preheat it to 250°F using hickory pellets or a mix.

8. Smoke the jalapeño peppers for one and a half to 2 hours at 250 ° F before the bacon is fried and crunchy.

9. Remove the ABTs from the grill and leave to rest before serving for 5 minutes.

3.2 Garlic Parmesan Wedges

Ready in about 45 minutes | Servings-3 | Difficulty-Moderate

Ingredients

- A quarter cup of extra-virgin olive oil
- 3⁄4 teaspoon of black pepper
- 3⁄4 cup of grated Parmesan cheese

- Three tablespoons of chopped fresh cilantro
- Three large russet potatoes
- One and a half teaspoons of salt
- Two teaspoons of garlic powder
- Half cup of blue cheese or ranch dressing per serving, for dipping (optional)

Instructions

1. Using a vegetable brush to gently clean the potatoes with cold water and allow the potatoes to dry.
2. Lengthwise, cut the potatoes in half and then split both halves into thirds.
3. To clean away all the humidity that is emitted as you cut the potatoes, use a paper towel. Moisture prevents the wedges from being crispy.
4. In a wide cup, put the potato wedges, pepper, salt, olive oil, and garlic powder and toss gently with your hands to ensure that the oil and spices are equally spread.
5. Arrange the wedges on a non-stick grilling tray/pan/basket on a single sheet.
6. For indirect cooking, set up your wood pellet smoker-grill and preheat it to 425 ° F using any form of wood pellet.
7. Place your preheated smoker-grill on the grilling tray and roast the potato wedges for Fifteen minutes before turning. Roast the potato wedges until the potatoes are fork-tender on the inside and crunchy golden brown on the outside, for an extra 15 to 20 minutes.
8. Sprinkle with Parmesan cheese on the potato wedges and garnish with, if needed, cilantro or parsley. If needed, serve with ranch dressing blue cheese for dipping.

3.3 Bacon-Wrapped Asparagus

Ready in about 45 minutes | Servings-4 to 6 | Difficulty-Hard

Ingredients

- Extra-virgin olive oil
- One pound of thick fresh asparagus
- Five slices of thinly sliced bacon
- One teaspoon of Pete's Western Rub
- Salt and pepper as per taste

Instructions

1. Snap and trim the woody ends of the asparagus so that they are both around the same weight.
2. Divide the asparagus into three-spear packets and spray it with olive oil. With one slice of bacon, seal each package and then sprinkle with the seasoning or salt and pepper to taste.
3. Configure your indirect cooking wood pellet smoker-grill, putting Teflon-coated fiberglass mats on top of the grates. Using some kind of pellets, preheat to 400°F. It is possible to preheat the grill when heating the asparagus.
4. For 25 to 30 minutes, grill the bacon-wrapped asparagus until the asparagus is soft and the bacon is fried and crispy.

3.4 Bourbon BBQ Smoked Chicken Wings

Ready in about 2 hours and 50 minutes | Servings-6 | Difficulty-Hard

Ingredients

Wings

- Sweet and smoky chicken rub or your favorite store-bought rub
- Four pounds of chicken wings
- Two tablespoons of vegetable oil

Bourbon BBQ Sauce

- Five finely minced cloves of garlic
- Half finely minced medium sweet yellow onion
- Half cup of bourbon
- A quarter cup of tomato paste
- Two cups of ketchup
- Half cup of packed light brown sugar
- 1/3 cup apple cider vinegar
- A quarter cup of Worcestershire sauce
- Two tablespoons of liquid smoke
- Half tablespoon of kosher salt
- Half teaspoon of black pepper
- A quarter teaspoon of cayenne pepper
- A few dashes of hot sauce (optional)

Instructions

For sauce

1. Over medium heat, add a drizzle of olive oil to a saucepan. Add the garlic and onion and cook for about 5 minutes. Add the bourbon and continue cooking for approximately 3 minutes.

2. To break it up, add tomato paste and whisk. Add all the remaining components of the sauce and whisk to combine. Increase the heat and bring it to a boil. Simmer for about 15-20 minutes and reduce the heat to medium-low or low.

3. When you like a smooth, glossy sauce, pour sauce through a fine-mesh sieve to strain out pieces of onion and garlic. Set aside to cool. Store the leftover BBQ sauce for 2-3 weeks in the refrigerator in an airtight container.

For wings

1. Pat dry chicken wings with a clean paper towel. In a large mixing bowl, add the wings and toss with the vegetable oil. Ensure that each wing is coated; add rub and massage into the wings.

2. Add pellets of hickory wood to the hopper. Turn on the smoker, open the lid and set the setting for the smoke. Smoke-free heat, lid open, 5-10 minutes, until very smoky. Set the smoker to 250 F degrees by adding chicken wings to the oiled grill grates. Close the smoker's lid and smoke for 2 hours and 30 minutes, or until the internal temperature of the chicken wings reaches 165 degrees F. To ensure precise cooking temperatures, use an instant reading meat thermometer.

3. With bourbon BBQ sauce, change the smoker setting to high and braise chicken wings on both sides. Cook the wings on the other side for 5 minutes, then flip them over and cook for 3-5 minutes.

4. To remove chicken wings from a foil or parchment coated plate or baking sheet, select Shut down on smoker. Allow 5-10 minutes to rest. Turn it off and unplug the smoker.

5. Eat the wings as they are, or brush them with extra BBQ sauce. Dip in the blue cheese or ranch dressing for a traditional experience and serve with celery and carrots.

3.5 Brisket Baked Beans

Ready in about 2 hours and 30 minutes | Servings-10 to 12 | Difficulty-Hard

Ingredients

- Two tablespoons of extra-virgin olive oil
- One large diced yellow onion,
- One medium diced green bell pepper
- One medium diced red bell pepper
- Two to six diced jalapeño peppers
- Three cups of chopped Texas-Style Brisket Flat
- One (28-ounce) can of baked beans, like Bush's Country Style Baked Beans
- One (28-ounce) can of pork and beans
- One (14-ounce) can of rinsed and drained red kidney beans
- One cup of barbecue sauce
- Half cup of packed brown sugar
- Three chopped garlic cloves
- Two teaspoons of ground mustard
- Half teaspoon of kosher salt
- Half teaspoon of black pepper

Instructions

1. Heat the olive oil in a skillet over medium heat, and then add the diced onion, peppers and jalapeños. Cook for about 8 to 10 minutes, occasionally stirring, until the onions are translucent.

2. Combine the chopped brisket, pork, baked beans and beans, cooked onion, kidney beans and peppers, barbecue sauce, brown sugar, ground mustard, garlic, black pepper and salt in a 4-quart casserole dish.

3. Use the pellets of choice to install your wood pellet smoker-grill for indirect cooking and preheat it to 325 ° F. Cook the uncovered brisket of baked beans for one and a half to 2 hours until the beans are dense and bubbly. Allow 15 minutes to rest before serving.

3.6 Crabmeat-Stuffed Mushrooms

Ready in about 50 minutes | Servings-4 to 6 | Difficulty-Moderate

Ingredients

- Extra-virgin olive oil
- Six medium portobello mushrooms
- 1⁄3 cup of grated Parmesan cheese

For the crabmeat stuffing

- Two tablespoons of extra-virgin olive oil
- Eight ounces of fresh crabmeat, or canned or imitation crab meat
- 1⁄3 cup of chopped celery
- 1⁄3 cup of chopped red bell pepper
- Half cup of chopped green onion
- Half cup of Italian bread crumbs
- Half cup of mayonnaise8 ounces cream cheese, at room temperature
- Half teaspoon of minced garlic
- One tablespoon of dried parsley

- Half cup of grated Parmesan cheese
- A quarter teaspoon of Old Bay seasoning
- A quarter teaspoon of kosher salt
- A quarter teaspoon of black pepper

Instructions

1. Using a damp paper towel, clean the mushroom caps. Cut and set aside the stems.
2. With a spoon, extract the brown gills from the undersides of the mushroom caps and dispose of them.
3. Get the crabmeat stuffing ready. Drain, rinse and remove any shell bits when using canned crabmeat.
4. Heat olive oil over medium-high heat in a skillet. Add the celery, green onion and bell pepper, and sauté for 5 minutes. Set to cool aside.
5. In a large bowl, mix the cooled sautéed vegetables gently with the rest of the ingredients.
6. Cover the crabmeat stuffing and refrigerate it until ready to use.
7. Fill the crab mixture with each mushroom cap, creating a mound in the center.
8. Sprinkle with extra-virgin olive oil and sprinkle the Parmesan cheese with each stuffed mushroom cap. In a 10 x, 15-inch baking dish, put the stuffed mushrooms.
9. Install your wood pellet smoker-grill for indirect heat and use any pellets to preheat to 375 ° F.
10. Bake for 30 to 45 minutes until the stuffing is hot and the mushrooms are beginning to release their juices (165 °F measured with an instant-read digital thermometer).

3.7 Hickory-Smoked Moink Ball Skewers

Ready in about 1 hour and 50 minutes | Servings-6 to 9 | Difficulty-Hard

Ingredients

- Half pound ground pork sausage
- Half pound ground beef
- One large egg
- Half cup of Italian bread crumbs
- Half cup of minced red onions
- Half cup of grated Parmesan cheese
- A quarter cup of finely chopped parsley
- A quarter cup of whole milk
- Two minced garlic cloves
- One teaspoon of oregano
- Half teaspoon of kosher salt
- Half teaspoon of black pepper
- Half pound thinly sliced bacon, cut in half
- A quarter cup of barbecue sauce

Instructions

1. Combine the ground pork sausage, ground beef, egg, onion, parmesan cheese, bread crumbs, parsley, milk, salt, garlic, oregano, and pepper in a large bowl. Don't overwork the flesh.
2. Form one and a half-ounce meatball, roughly 1 inch in diameter, and place them on a fiberglass mat coated with Teflon.

3. Wrap half a slice of thin bacon with each meatball. On six skewers, spear the moink balls (3 balls per skewer)

4. For indirect cooking, configure your wood pellet smoker-grill.

5. Using hickory pellets, preheat your wood pellet smoker-grill to 225°F.

6. For 30 minutes, smoke the Moink Ball Skewers.

7. Raise the pit temperature to 350 ° F until the internal temperature of the meatballs reaches 175 ° F, and the bacon is crunchy (approximately 40 to 45 minutes).

8. During the last 5 minutes, brush the moink balls with your favourite barbecuing sauce.

3.8 Smashed Potato Casserole

Ready in about 1 hour and 55 minutes|Servings-8| Difficulty-Hard

Ingredients

- A quarter cup of (Half stick) salted butter
- Ten bacon slices
- One small thinly sliced red onion
- One small thinly green sliced bell pepper
- One small thinly sliced red bell pepper
- One small thinly sliced yellow bell pepper
- Three cups of mashed potatoes
- 3⁄4 cup of sour cream
- One and a half teaspoons of Texas Barbecue Rub
- Four cups of frozen hash brown potatoes
- Three cups of shredded sharp cheddar cheese

Instructions

1. Over medium heat, cook the bacon in a large skillet until crisp, about 5 minutes on each side. Set aside the bacon.
2. To a glass container, transfer the rendered bacon grease.
3. Warm the butter or bacon grease in the same large skillet, over medium heat, and sauté the red onion and bell peppers until al dente. Just set aside.
4. Spray non-stick cooking spray on a 9 to 11-inch casserole dish and spread the mashed potatoes on the bottom of the dish.
5. Layer the sour cream and season with Texas Barbecue Rub over the mashed potatoes.
6. On top of the potatoes, layer the sautéed vegetables and keep the butter or bacon grease in the pan.
7. Sprinkle with half a cup of sharp cheddar cheese, followed by brown potatoes with frozen hash.
8. Spoon over the hash browns with the residual butter or bacon fat from the sautéed vegetables and top with crumbled bacon.
9. Top with one and a half of the remaining cups of sharp cheddar cheese and cover with a lid or aluminium foil over the casserole dish.
10. Use the pellets of choice to customize your wood pellet smoker-grill for indirect cooking and preheat it to 350 ° F.
11. For 45 to 60 minutes, bake the mashed potato casserole until the cheese is bubbling.
12. Before serving, let it rest for 10 minutes.

3.9 Roasted Vegetables

Ready in about 1 hour | Servings-4 | Difficulty-Moderate

Ingredients

- One cup of small halved mushrooms
- One medium sliced and halved yellow squash
- One small chopped red onion
- Six medium stemmed asparagus spears
- A quarter cup of roasted garlic–flavoured extra-virgin olive oil
- Three minced garlic cloves
- One teaspoon of dried oregano
- Half teaspoon of black pepper
- One cup of cauliflower florets
- One medium sliced and halved zucchini
- One medium chopped red bell pepper
- Six ounces of small baby carrots
- One cup of cherry or grape tomatoes
- Two tablespoons of balsamic vinegar
- One teaspoon of dried thyme
- One teaspoon of garlic salt

Instructions

1. Place in a large bowl the florets of cauliflower, mushrooms, yellow squash, red bell pepper, zucchini, carrots and red onions, tomatoes and asparagus.
2. Stir in the vegetables with olive oil, garlic, balsamic vinegar, thyme, oregano, black pepper and garlic salt

3. Toss the vegetables gently with your hand until they are fully encased with olive oil, herbs, and spices.

4. Spread the seasoned vegetables evenly on a non-stick grilling tray/pan/basket

5. For indirect cooking, set up your wood pellet smoker-grill and preheat it to 425 ° F using any form of wood pellet.

6. To the preheated smoker-grill, transfer the grilling tray and roast the vegetables for 20 to 40 minutes, or until the veggies are al dente. Immediately serve.

3.10 Applewood-Smoked Cheese

Ready in about 3 hours |Servings-Many| Difficulty-Hard

Ingredients

One-to-two and a half-pound block of the following suggested cheeses like

- Sharp cheddar
- Gouda
- Extra-sharp 3-year cheddar
- Pepper Jack Swiss
- Monterey Jack

Instructions

1. Break the cheese blocks into compact sizes to maximize smoke penetration based on the form of the cheese blocks.

2. To allow a very thin skin or crust to develop that serves as a barrier to heat but enables the smoke to enter, let the cheese sit uncovered on the counter for 1 hour.

3. Mount a cold-smoke package to customize your wood pellet smoker-grill for indirect fire and plan for cold-smoking.

4. Ensure that the louver vents of the smoker box are completely open to allow the box to avoid moisture.

5. Preheat your smoker-grill wood pellet to 180 ° F, or if you have one, use the smoke mode, using apple pellets for a milder smoke taste.

6. Put the cheese on non-stick grill mats of Teflon-coated fiberglass and cold-smoke for 2 hours.

7. Take the smoked cheese and use a cooling rack to allow it to cool on the counter for an hour.

8. Vacuum-seal and mark your smoked cheeses for a minimum of 2 weeks before refrigerating to enable the smoke to absorb and mellow the cheese's taste.

3.11 Bacon Cheddar Sliders

Ready in 45 minutes | Servings-6 to 10 | Difficulty-Moderate

Ingredients

- Half teaspoon of garlic salt
- Half teaspoon of garlic powder
- Half teaspoon of black pepper
- Half cup of mayonnaise
- Six (1-ounce) slices of sharp cheddar cheese, cut in half
- One and a half pounds ground beef
- Half teaspoon of seasoned salt
- Half teaspoon of onion powder
- Six bacon slices, cut in half

- Two teaspoons of creamy horseradish
- Half small red onion, thinly sliced
- Ketchup
- Half cup of sliced kosher dill pickles12 mini buns

Instructions

1. In a medium dish, blend together the ground beef, seasoned salt, garlic salt, garlic powder, black pepper and onion powder
2. Divide the meat mixture into 12 equal portions and form them into small, thin, circular patties and set aside (approximately 2 ounces each).
3. Over medium pressure, cook the bacon in a medium skillet until crisp, around 5 to 8 minutes. Only put back.
4. Mix the mayonnaise and horseradish, if used, in a wide bowl to render the sauce. In order to use a griddle accessory, customize your wood pellet smoker-grill for direct cooking. Check with your supplier
5. And see if they have a griddle accessory that fits your special smoker-grill for wood pellets.
6. For better non-stick results, coat the griddle's cooking surface with cooking spray.
7. Using the pellets of your choosing, preheat your wood pellet smoker-grill to 350°F. Your griddle's surface should be around 400°F.
8. Grill the patties on either side for 3 to 4 minutes before they are cooked to an internal temperature of 160°F.
9. If needed, put on each patty a slice of sharp cheddar cheese while the patty is still on the griddle or after the patty has been removed from the griddle. On the

bottom half of each roll, put a dollop of the mayonnaise mixture, a red slice of onion, and a burger patty. Pickle slices, sausage, and ketchup on top.

3.12 Teriyaki Steak Bites

Ready in 1 hour and 45 minutes | Servings-4 | Difficulty-Moderate

Ingredients

- Teriyaki Marinade
- One tablespoon of light brown sugar packed
- One teaspoon of garlic salt
- Two pounds of top sirloin steak
- A quarter cup of teriyaki sauce
- One teaspoon of garlic powder
- One tablespoon of soy sauce
- Half teaspoon of pepper
- One tablespoon of apple cider vinegar

Instructions

1. Mix all of the marinade components together in a tiny mixing bowl.
2. Trim the steak and split it into 2-inch bits. Place in the Ziploc bag and add in the steak top marinade. Squeeze out as much air as you can and lock the jar. Put in the fridge for a period of 8 hours or overnight.
3. The steak bites are prepared to be smoked to 225 degrees according to the instructions of the maker until ready to smoke.

4. Place it on the smoker grates or on a rack right away. Remove the leftover marinade. Smoke for 1 hour and 30 minutes or until 135-140 degrees F is the internal temperature. Remove from the smoker and quickly serve.

Chapter 4-Lunch Recipes

4.1 Jan's Grilled Quarters

Ready in about 2 hours and 15 minutes (marination time excluded) |Servings-4| Difficulty-Hard

Ingredients

- Four fresh or thawed frozen chicken quarters
- Four tablespoons of Jan's Original Dry Rub
- Four to Six tablespoons of extra-virgin olive oil

Instructions

1. Trim any extra skin and fat off the chicken parts. Peel the chicken skin gently and rub the olive oil on and under each quarter of the chicken skin.
2. Season with Jan's Initial Dry Rub on and below the skins and on the backs of the chicken parts.
3. To allow the flavors time to absorb, seal the seasoned chicken pieces in plastic wrap and refrigerate for 2 to 4 hours.

4. Customize your wood pellet smoker-grill for indirect cooking and use some pellets to preheat to 325 ° F.

5. On the barbecue, position the chicken quarters and cook at 325 ° F for 1 hour.

6. To finish the chicken quarters and crisp the skins, lift the pit temperature to 400 ° F after an hour.

7. When the interior temperature, at the thickest areas of the thighs and legs, exceeds 180 ° F, take the crispy chicken quarters off the grill, and the juices flow out.

8. Until eating, rest the grilled spicy chicken quarters under a loose foil tent for 15 minutes.

4.2 Cajun Spatchcock Chicken

Ready in about 3 hours 20 minutes (marination time excluded) |Servings-4| Difficulty-Hard

Ingredients

- Four to five-pound fresh or thawed frozen young chicken
- Four tablespoons of Cajun Spice Rub
- Four to Six tablespoons of extra-virgin olive oil

Instructions

1. Set the breast-side chicken down on a cutting board.

2. In order to extract it, cut down both sides of the backbone using kitchen or poultry shears.

3. To flatten it, turn the chicken over and push tightly down on the breast. Loosen the skin of the breast, thigh, and drumstick gently and peel it down.

4. Apply the olive oil liberally under and on the skin. Season the chicken under the skin on both sides and directly over the flesh.

5. To allow the flavors time to absorb, cover the chicken in plastic wrap and let it sit for 3 hours in the refrigerator.

6. For indirect cooking, customize your wood pellet smoker-grill and preheat it to 225°F using hickory, pecan pellets, or a mix.

7. For an hour and a half, smoke the chicken.

8. Increase the pit temperature to 375 ° F after one and a half hours at 225 ° F, and roast until the internal temperature at the thickest section of the breast exceeds 170 ° F and the thighs are at least 180 ° F.

9. Until slicing, rest the chicken under a loose foil tent for 15 minutes.

4.3 Smoked Pork Tenderloins

Ready in about 2 hours (marination time excluded) |Servings-6| Difficulty-Hard

Ingredients

- Two pork tenderloins (one and a half to two pounds)
- A quarter cup of Jan's Original Dry Rub or Pork Dry Rub
- A quarter cup of roasted garlic–flavored extra-virgin olive oil

Instructions

1. Trim all of the meat's extra fat and silver skin.

2. Apply with olive oil and dust both sides of the tenderloins with the rub.3. For 2 to 4 hours, seal the seasoned tenderloins in plastic wrap and refrigerate.

3. For indirect cooking, set up your wood pellet smoker-grill and preheat it to 230°F utilizing hickory or apple pellets.

4. Take off the plastic wrap from the meat and place the smoker-grill probes of your wood pellet or a remote meat probe into the thickest section of each tenderloin. If your grill does not have meat probe capability or if you do not have a remote meat

probe, use a wireless instant-read thermometer for internal temperature readings during the cooker.

5. Set the tenderloins directly on the grill and smoke them at 230 ° F for 45 minutes.

6. Increase the temperature of the pit to 350 ° F and finish cooking the tenderloins for around 45 more minutes until the interior temperature exceeds 145 ° F at the thickest stage.

7. Until cooking, rest the pork tenderloins under a thin foil tent for 10 minutes.

4.4 Pellet Grill Smokehouse Burger

Ready in about 1 hour 30 minutes |Servings-6| Difficulty-Hard

Ingredients

- Two pounds of ground chuck
- One tablespoon of paprika
- One and a half teaspoons of kosher salt
- Six thick-cut bacon slices
- One tablespoon of soy sauce
- One medium-sized red onion
- Six Kaiser rolls
- Six tablespoons ketchup
- A quarter cup of Dijon mustard
- Two teaspoons of onion powder
- One and a half teaspoons of black pepper
- A quarter cup of unsalted butter
- One tablespoon of Worcestershire sauce

- Six sharp Cheddar cheese slices
- ¾ cup mayonnaise
- Hickory hardwood pellets

Instructions

1. In compliance with the manufacturer's guidance, fill a pellet jar with hardwood pellets into an electronic pellet grill. Set the temperature of the pellet grill to 415 °F, close the lid and preheat for 10 to 15 minutes.
2. In a big tub, blend the beef, paprika, mustard, garlic powder, onion powder, pepper and salt together. Form into six patties (4-inch-wide).
3. In a broad cast-iron or another heat-resistant pan, place the bacon and place it on the grill grate. Close the lid and grill for 25 to 30 minutes until the bacon is mostly crisp and most of the fat is made. Take the bacon out of the pan and drain it on paper towels. Drain skillet drippings; do not wipe clean skillet.
4. Melt the butter on the grill in a pan. To the skillet, add soy sauce and Worcestershire sauce, then mix to blend. Attach the onions to the skillet and position them on one side of the grill. Place the patties and shut the cover on the other side. Grill before a meat thermometer is placed from 130 ° F to 135 ° F in patty registers, 7 1/2 to 10 minutes per hand. Top the patties with slices of cheese, cover, and barbecue for 1 to 2 minutes before the cheese is melted. Put the buns on the grill, cut side down, and grill for around 1 minute until toasted.
5. Uniformly distributed mayonnaise and ketchup on sliced sides of buns. Place bun bottoms with patties, bacon, and onions; cover with tops, and serve immediately.

4.5 Roasted Leg of Lamb

Ready in about 2 hours 30 minutes (marination time excluded) |Servings-8| Difficulty-Hard

Ingredients

- Half cup of roasted garlic–flavored extra-virgin olive oil
- Three minced garlic cloves
- Two tablespoons of dried oregano
- Half teaspoon of black pepper
- One (Four pounds) boneless leg of lamb
- A quarter cup of dried parsley
- Two tablespoons of fresh-squeezed lemon juice or one tablespoon of lemon zest
- One tablespoon of dried rosemary

Instructions

1. Remove some netting from the lamb's leg. Trim off any wide bits of gristle, fat, and silver skin.
2. Mix the olive oil, garlic, parsley, lemon juice or zest, rosemary, oregano and pepper in a shallow dish.
3. On the inner and outer surfaces of the boneless leg of the lamb, add a spice rub.
4. To protect the boneless leg of lamb, use silicone food-grade cooking bands or butcher's twine. To build and retain the simple shape of the lamb, use bands or twine.

5. Cover the lamb loosely with plastic wrap and chill overnight to allow the meat to penetrate the seasonings.

6. Take the lamb from the fridge and let it stand for an hour at room temperature.

7. Use the pellets of choice to rig your wood pellet smoker-grill for indirect cooking and preheat it to 400 ° F.

8. Break the lamb's plastic wrap.

9. Insert the thickest portion of the lamb with your wood pellet smoker-grill meat probe or a remote meat probe. If your grill does not have meat probe capability or if you do not have a remote meat probe, use a wireless instant-read thermometer for internal temperature readings during the cooker. At 400 °F, roast the lamb until the internal temperature exceeds the ideal doneness at the thickest section.

10. Until cutting against the grain and cooking, rest the lamb under a loose foil tent for 10 minutes.

4.6 Teriyaki Smoked Drumsticks

Ready in about 2 hours 30 minutes (marination time excluded) |Servings-4| Difficulty-Hard

Ingredients

- Three teaspoons of Poultry Seasoning
- Ten chicken drumsticks
- Three cups of teriyaki marinade and cooking sauce
- One teaspoon of garlic powder

Instructions

1. Mix the cooking sauce and marinade with the poultry seasoning and garlic powder in a medium bowl.

2. To facilitate marinade penetration, peel back the skin on the drumsticks.3. Place the drumsticks in a marinating pan or 1-gallon sealable plastic bag and pour over the drumsticks the marinade mixture. Overnight, refrigerate.

3. Rotate the morning chicken drumsticks.

4. Configure the indirect cooking of your wood pellet smoker grill.

5. To drain on a cooking sheet on your counter while the grill is preheating, replace the skin over the drumsticks and hang the drumsticks on a poultry leg-and-wing rack. If you don't own a poultry leg-and-wing rack, you can use paper towels to lightly pat the drumsticks dry.

6. Using hickory or maple pellets, preheat your wood pellet smoker-grill to 180°F.

7. Marinated chicken drumsticks should be smoked for 1 hour.

8. Increase the pit temperature to 350 ° F after an hour and cook the drumsticks for a further 30 to 45 minutes before the interior temperature of the thickest section of the drumsticks exceeds 180 ° F.

9. Before serving, rest the chicken drumsticks under a loose foil tent for 15 minutes.

4.7 Applewood Walnut-Crusted Rack of Lamb

Ready in about 2 hours (marination time excluded) |Servings-4| Difficulty-Hard

Ingredients

- Two minced garlic cloves
- Half teaspoon of kosher salt

- Half teaspoon of rosemary
- One cup of crushed walnuts
- Three tablespoons of Dijon mustard
- Half teaspoon of garlic powder
- Half teaspoon of black pepper
- One rack of lamb (one to two pounds)

Instructions

1. In a small bowl, combine the garlic, mustard, garlic powder, pepper, salt, and rosemary together.
2. Spread evenly on all sides of the lamb with the seasoning mix and sprinkle with the crushed walnuts. To stick the nuts to the meat, press the walnuts lightly with your hand.
3. Wrap the walnut-crusted lamb rack loosely with plastic wrap and cool overnight to allow the meat to penetrate the seasonings.
4. To allow it to reach room temperature, remove the walnut-crusted rack of lamb from the refrigerator and let it relax for 30 minutes.
5. For indirect cooking, configure your wood pellet smoker-grill and preheat it to 225 ° F using apple pellets.
6. Put the bone-side lamb rack down directly on the grill.
7. Smoke at 225 ° F until the thickest part of the lamb rack, measured with a digital instant-read thermometer, reaches the desired internal temperature as you are near the times listed in the chart.
8. Before serving, rest the lamb under a loose foil tent for 5 minutes.

4.8 Hot-Smoked Teriyaki Tuna

Ready in about 9 hours 10 minutes | Servings-4 | Difficulty-Hard

Ingredients

- Two cups of Mr. Yoshida's Traditional Teriyaki Marinade and Cooking Sauce
- Two (10-ounce) fresh tuna steaks

Instructions

1. Slice the tuna into slices that are uniformly thick, about 2 inches thick.
2. Place the tuna slices along with the marinade in a 1-gallon sealable plastic bag and place it in a shallow baking dish in case of a leak. Let the tuna rotate every hour and sit in the refrigerator for 3 hours.
3. Remove the tuna from the marinade after 3 hours and lightly pat it dry with a paper towel.
4. Enable the tuna to air-dry for 2 to 4 hours in the refrigerator, uncovered, until pellicles form.
5. For indirect cooking, configure your wood pellet smoker-grill and preheat it to 180 ° F using alder pellets.
6. On a Teflon-coated fiberglass mat or directly on the grill grates, place the tuna pieces, and smoke the tuna for an hour.
7. Increase the temperature of the pit to 250°F after 1 hour. Cook for another 1 hour until the internal temperature reaches 145 degrees F.
8. Remove the tuna from the grill and leave to rest before serving for 10 minutes.

4.9 Baked Fresh Wild Sockeye Salmon

Ready in about 40 minutes | Servings-6 | Difficulty-Moderate

Ingredients

- Two fresh wild sockeye salmon fillets
- 3⁄4 teaspoon of Old Bay seasoning
- Two teaspoons of Seafood Seasoning

Instructions

1. Rinse the salmon fillets with cool water and wipe them dry with a paper towel.
2. Lightly brush the fillets with the seasonings.
3. Customize your wood pellet smoker-grill for indirect cooking and preheat to 400°F using some pellets.
4. Lay the skin-side down of salmon on a Teflon-coated fiberglass mat or directly on the grill grates.
5. Bake the salmon for 15 to 20 minutes before the internal temperature exceeds 140°F, and/or the meat flakes easily with a fork.
6. Rest the salmon for 5 minutes before eating.

4.10 Bacon Cordon Bleu

Ready in about 3 hours 15 minutes | Servings-6 | Difficulty-Hard

Ingredients

- Three large skinless and butterflied boneless chicken breasts
- Three tablespoons of Jan's Original Dry Rub or Poultry Seasoning
- Twelve slices of provolone cheese
- Twenty-four bacon slices
- Three tablespoons of roasted garlic–flavored extra-virgin olive oil

- Twelve slices of black forest ham

Instructions

1. Weave four bacon slices closely together, leaving extra room at the ends. Alternate bacon slices are interlocked by the bacon weave and used to wind around the chicken cordon bleu.
2. Spritz or brush two thin chicken breast fillets on both sides with olive oil.
3. With the seasoning, clean all sides of the chicken breast fillets.
4. On the bacon weave, plate one seasoned chicken fillet and finish with one slice of each ham and Provolone cheese.
5. Using another chicken fillet, ham, and cheese, repeat the operation. Fold in half the chicken, ham and cheese.
6. To cover the chicken cordon blue fully, overlap the bacon strips from opposite ends.
7. To keep the bacon strips in place, use silicone food-grade cooking bands, butcher's twine, or toothpicks.
8. For the leftover chicken breasts and ingredients, repeat the procedure.
9. Configure your wood pellet smoker-grill with apple or cherry pellets for indirect cooking and preheating for smoking (180 ° F to 200 ° F).
10. For 1 hour, smoke the bacon cordon bleu.
11. Increase the pit temperature to 350°F after smoking for an hour.
12. If the internal temperature exceeds 165 ° F and the bacon is crisp, the bacon cordon bleu is cooked.
13. Until eating, rest under a loose foil tent for 15 minutes.

4.11 Pulled Hickory-smoked Pork Butts

Ready in about 11 hours (marination time excluded) |Servings-20 or more| Difficulty-Hard

Ingredients

- Two (10-pound) boneless pork butts, vacuum-packed or fresh
- 3⁄4 cup of Pork Dry Rub, Jan's Original Dry Rub or your favorite pork rub
- One cup of roasted garlic–flavored extra-virgin olive oil

Instructions

1. If you see fit, take off the fat cap and any readily accessible broad portions of surplus fat from each pork ass. Some tend to reduce the fat cap to a quarter of an inch or keep the whole fat cap on because they assume that when they roast, the melting fat bastes the butts. In areas protected by fat, this process prevents the development of bark.
2. Break each butt of pork in half. To keep the meat intact through cooking and handling, use silicone food-grade cooking bands or butcher's twine.
3. Rub the oil over all the sides of each pork ass. Sprinkle a liberal sum of the rub with each pork butt and pat it with your fist.
4. The seasoned boneless pork butts are individually double-wrapped in plastic wrap and refrigerated overnight.
5. For indirect cooking, set up your wood pellet smoker-grill and preheat it to 225 ° F utilizing hickory pellets.
6. Takedown the pork butts from the refrigerator and, when preheating your wood pellet smoker-grill, remove the plastic wrap.

7. There's no need for pork butts to totally hit room temperature. In the thickest section of one or more pork butts, place your wood pellet smoker-grill meat probes or a remote meat probe. If your grill does not have meat probe capability or you do not possess a remote meat probe, for internal temperature measurements, use an instant-read wireless thermometer during the cook.3. Smoke the butts of pork for 3 hours.

8. Increase the pit temperature to 350 °F after 3 hours and cook before the butts' internal temperature exceeds 160 °F.

9. Take the butts of pork from the barbecue and cover each one in heavy-duty aluminum foil twice. Take caution to ensure that when you double-wrap them, you hold the meat probes in the butts.

10. To your 350°F pellet smoker-grill, return the wrapped pork butts.

11. Until the internal temperature of the pork butts exceeds 200 ° to 205 ° F, continue cooking the foil-wrapped pork butts.

12. Prior to pulling and cooking, remove the pork butts and FTC for 3 to 4 hours.

13. Using your preferred pulling tool, pull the smoked pork butts into little succulent shreds.

14. Mix the pulled pork butts with any remaining liquid if you'd like. On a fresh-baked roll topped with coleslaw, serve the pulled pork with barbecue sauce or serve the pulled pork with condiments such as lettuce, tomato, red onion, mayo, horseradish and cheese.

4.12 Pellet Grill Pork Loin with Salsa Verde

Ready in about 1 hour 15 minutes |Servings-8| Difficulty-Hard

Ingredients

Salsa Verde

- Half cup of finely chopped shallots
- ⅓ cup chopped fresh cilantro
- One tablespoon of chopped capers
- One teaspoon of grated garlic
- One teaspoon of kosher salt
- Four chopped anchovy fillets
- One cup of olive oil
- ⅓ cup of chopped fresh flat-leaf parsley
- A quarter cup of chopped fresh dill
- One teaspoon of grated lemon zest
- One teaspoon of grated fresh ginger
- ¾ teaspoon crushed red pepper

Pork Loin

- Two teaspoons of kosher salt
- Three tablespoons of fresh lemon juice
- Three and a half pounds boneless
- One teaspoon of black pepper

Instructions

1. Prepare Salsa Verde: In a medium dish, stir together all the ingredients. Just set aside.
2. Prepare the Pork Loin: Fill a pellet jar with hardwood pellets on an electric pellet grill as instructed by the maker. Set the temperature of the pellet grill to 350

°F, close the lid and preheat for 10 to 15 minutes. Sprinkle the pork with salt and pepper all around.

3. Place the pork on the grill, close the lid, and grill on both sides until lightly browned, about 7 1/2 minutes per side. Spin the pork up with the fat cap if necessary, and finish with half the Salsa Verde. Cover the lid and barbecue for 25 to 30 minutes before a meat thermometer inserted into the thickest part registers 140 ° F.

4. Take the pork off the grill and let it sit for 15 minutes before slicing. Mix the lemon juice and the remaining Salsa Verde together, and spoon over the sliced pork.

Chapter 5-Dinner Recipes

5.1 Roasted Tuscan Thighs

Ready in about 1 hour and 45 minutes (marination time excluded) |Servings-4| Difficulty-Hard

Ingredients

- Eight chicken thighs
- Three teaspoons of Tuscan Seasoning or any Tuscan seasoning, per thigh
- Three tablespoons of roasted garlic–flavored extra-virgin olive oil

Instructions

1. Trim any extra skin from the chicken thighs to prepare for shrinkage, preserving a quarter of an inch.
2. Peel back the skin gently to clear any large fat deposits under the skin and on the back of the leg.
3. Apply the olive oil gently on and under the skin and back of the thighs. Season with Tuscan seasoning on and below the surface and back of the thighs.

4. To allow the flavors time to absorb before roasting, seal the chicken thighs in plastic wrap and refrigerate for 1 to 2 hours.

5. Configure your wood pellet smoker-grill for indirect cooking and use some pellets to preheat to 375 ° F.

6. Roast the chicken thighs for 40 to 60 minutes, depending on your wood pellet smoker-grill, before the internal temperature at the thickest section of the thighs exceeds 180 ° F. Until eating, rest the roasted Tuscan thighs under a loose foil tent for 15 minutes.

5.2 Smoked Bone-In Turkey Breast

Ready in about 5 hours | Servings-6 to 8 | Difficulty-Hard

Ingredients

- One (eight to ten pound) bone-in turkey breast
- Five tablespoons of Jan's Original Dry Rub or Poultry Seasoning
- Six tablespoons of extra-virgin olive oil

Instructions

1. Trim away some extra turkey breast fat and skin.
2. Separate the skin from the breast cautiously, keeping the skin preserved. Within the breast hollow, under the skin and on the skin, apply the olive oil.
3. Season the breast cavity generously with rub or seasoning, under the surface, and on the skin.
4. Place the turkey breast, breast-side up, in a V-rack for better handling or directly on the grill grates.
5. Enable the turkey breast on your kitchen countertop to rest at room temperature when preheating your wood pellet smoker barbecue.

6. For indirect cooking, set your wood pellet smoker-grill and preheat it to 225°F utilizing hickory or pecan pellets.

7. For 2 hours, smoke the bone-in turkey breast at 225 °F on the V-rack or directly on the grill grates.

8. Elevate the temperature of the pit to 325 ° F after 2 hours of hickory smoke. Roast until an internal temperature of 170 ° F hits the thickest section of the turkey breast, and the juices run clear.

9. Before cutting against the grain, rest the hickory-smoked turkey breast under a loose foil tent for 20 minutes.

5.3 Crab-Stuffed Lemon Cornish Hens

Ready in about 2 hours 15 minutes (marination time excluded) |Servings-2 to 4| Difficulty-Hard

Ingredients

- Two Cornish hens
- Four tablespoons of Pete's Western Rub or any poultry rub
- One halved lemon
- Two cups of Crabmeat Stuffing

Instructions

1. Rinse the hens inside and out vigorously and pat off. Loosen the breast and leg skin cautiously. Under and on the skin and inside the cavity, rub the lemon. Rub the Western Pete's Rub under and on the skin of the breast and thigh. Return the skin to its original location cautiously.

2. To allow the flavors time to mature, seal the Cornish hens in plastic wrap and refrigerate for 2 to 3 hours.

3. Prepare according to the guidelines for the Crabmeat Stuffing. Before stuffing the hens, make sure it has cooled absolutely. Stuff each hen cavity loosely with the crab stuffing.
4. To hold the stuffing in, bind the Cornish hen legs together with butcher's twine.
5. Set your wood pellet smoker-grill with some pellets for indirect cooking and preheat to 375 ° F.
6. Place the stuffed hens inside a baking dish on a shelf. If you don't have a rack small enough to match, you may also directly position the hens in the baking bowl.
7. The hens are roasted at 375 ° F until the internal temperature exceeds 170 ° F at the thickest section of the breast, the thighs exceed 180 ° F, and the juices run clear.
8. To see if it has hit a temperature of 165°F, measure the crabmeat stuffing.
9. Until eating, rest the roasted hens under a loose foil tent for 15 minutes.

5.4 Double-Smoked Ham

Ready in about 2 hours | Servings-8 to 12 | Difficulty-Hard

Ingredients

- One (ten pounds) applewood-smoked, boneless, fully cooked, ready-to-eat ham or bone-in smoked ham

Instructions

1. Take the ham from its wrapping and allow to rest for 30 minutes at room temperature.
2. Depending on what kind of wood was used for the initial smoking, customize your wood pellet smoker-grill for indirect cooking and preheat it to 180°F using apple or hickory pellets.

3. Directly put the ham on the grill grates and smoke the ham at 180°F for 1 hour.

4. Elevate the pit temperature to 350 ° F after an hour.

5. Cook the ham for around one and a half to 2 more hours before the internal temperature exceeds 140 ° F.

6. Until cutting against the grain, cut the ham and cover it in foil for 15 minutes.

5.5 Easy No-Fail Pellet Smoker Ribs

Ready in about 6 hours | Servings-4 | Difficulty-Hard

Ingredients

- Two racks of Baby Back or Spare Ribs
- BBQ Rib Rub

Instructions

1. Begin preheating your pellet smoker at 225 degrees F as you are prepping the ribs. Following the directions and start-up procedure of your pellet smoker brand is critical.

2. Ribs normally come on the underside of the rack with a thin coat of rough muscle. This is known as the silver skin, and it has to be extracted so that the meat can penetrate the seasonings.

3. On a sheet tray, put the ribs and apply around 2-3 tablespoons of rib rub each hand. You don't want to coat them fully to make any of the meat peek in.

4. You may position the rack (or two racks) directly on the grates until the smoker is preheated and let them burn. Leave them for at least 4 hours alone. The shorter you open your barbecue, the shorter your cooking period would be. You

ought to keep an eye on the temperature of the smoker to ensure it remains where it is placed.

5. It will take 4 or 5 hours for a rack of baby back ribs to cook, and it will take 6 to 7 hours for spare ribs.

6. Pick up the ribs with tongs at the end of the cooking time, and if the bark splits and the ribs are nearly cut in two, they are cooked. Keep on smoking if not.

7. Add sauce to the BBQ. You should cover them with a thin film of your preferred BBQ sauce when the ribs are about to come out of the smoker (they passed the bending test). For 30 more minutes, keep them on the smoker at 225 degrees F so that the sauce will caramelize.

5.6 Texas-Style Brisket Flat

Ready in about 10 hours 45 minutes | Servings-8 to 10 | Difficulty-Hard

Ingredients

- Six and a Half pound beef brisket flat
- Half cup of Texas-Style Brisket Rub or your favorite brisket rub
- Half cup of roasted garlic–flavored extra-virgin olive oil

Instructions

1. Trim the brisket's fat cap off and extract any silver skin.2. Rub the trimmed meat with olive oil on both ends.

2. Apply the rub on both sides of the brisket, making sure that the rub is thoroughly coated.

3. Double-cover the brisket in plastic wrap and refrigerate overnight to reach the beef with the rub, or you can quickly sear the brisket if you choose.

4. Take the brisket from the fridge and put the smoker-grill wood pellet or a remote meat probe into the thickest portion of the meat. If you don't have a meat probe, capabilities or a remote meat probe on your barbecue, then use an instant-read optical thermometer for internal temperature readings during the cooker.
5. For indirect cooking, set up your wood pellet smoker-grill and preheat it to 250 ° F using mesquite or oak pellets.
6. At 250°F, smoke the brisket before the inner temperature exceeds 160°F (about 4 hours).
7. Remove the grill from the brisket, double-wrap it in heavy-duty aluminum foil, make sure the meat probe is left in place, and add it to the grill for smokers.
8. Increase the temperature of the pit to 325 ° F, then cook the brisket for another 2 hours before the internal temperature exceeds 205 ° F.
9. The foiled brisket is cut, wrapped in a cloth, and put in a cooler. Let sit 2 to 4 hours in the cooler before slicing against the grain and serving.

5.7 Hickory-Smoked Prime Rib of Pork

Ready in about 4 hours 15 minutes (marination time excluded) |Servings-6| Difficulty-Hard

Ingredients

- One (Five pounds) rack of pork, about six ribs
- Six tablespoons of Jan's Original Dry Rub, Pork Dry Rub or your favorite pork roast rub
- A quarter cup of roasted garlic–flavored extra-virgin olive oil

Instructions

1. Trim the fat cap and silver skin off the pork rack. A rack of pork has a membrane on the bones, much like a slice of ribs. Using a spoon handle under the bone membrane to loosen the membrane from the bones so you can reach the membrane with a paper towel to take it off.

2. On both sides of the beef, rub the olive oil liberally. Season with the seasoning, coating the beef on both sides. 3. The seasoned rack of pork is double covered in plastic wrap and refrigerated for 2 to 4 hours or overnight.

3. Take the seasoned pork rack from the refrigerator and let it rest for 30 minutes before cooking at room temperature.

4. For indirect cooking, set up your wood pellet smoker-grill and preheat it to 225 ° F utilizing hickory pellets.

5. Insert into the thickest portion of the rack of pork the wood pellet smoker-grill meat probe or a remote meat probe. Using an instant-read wireless thermometer while cooking for internal temperature readings if your grill does not have meat probe capability or you do not have a remote meat probe.

6. Set the rib-side of the rack down directly on the grill grates.

7. For 3 to 3 and a half hours, smoke the pork rack before the internal temperature exceeds 140 ° F.

8. Remove from the smoker's meat and let it rest 15 minutes before being carved under a loose foil tent.

5.8 Meaty Chuck Short Ribs

Ready in about 6 hours 35 minutes |Servings- 2 to 4| Difficulty-Hard

Ingredients

- English-cut 4-bone slab beef chuck short ribs

- Three to five tablespoons of Pete's Western Rub
- Three to four tablespoons of yellow mustard or extra-virgin olive oil

Instructions

1. Remove some silver skin by trimming the fat cap off the ribs, leaving a quarter of an inch of fat.
2. To season the meat correctly by working a spoon handle under the membrane to get a slice raised, separate the membrane from the bones. To catch the membrane, use a paper towel to take it off the bones.
3. Slather both sides of the short rib slab with mustard or olive oil. With the rub, season liberally on both edges.
4. Using mesquite or hickory pellets, set up your wood pellet smoker-grill for indirect heat and preheat to 225 ° F.
5. In the thickest section of the slab of ribs, place your wood pellet smoker-grill or a remote meat probe. If your grill does not have meat probe capability or you do not have a remote meat probe, then for internal temperature measurements, use an instant-read optical thermometer during the cooker.
6. On the grill, put the short ribs bone-side down and smoke for 5 hours at 225 ° F.
7. If the ribs have not achieved an internal temperature of at least 195 ° F after 5 hours, so the pit temperature can rise to 250 ° F before the inner temperature exceeds 195 °F to 205 ° F.
8. Until eating, rest the smoked short ribs under a loose foil tent for 15 minutes.

5.9 Roasted Duck à I' Orange

Ready in about 3 hours and 50 minutes | Servings-3 to 4 | Difficulty-Hard

Ingredients

- One (Five to six-pound) frozen Long Island, Peking, or Canadian duck
- One large orange, cut into wedges
- Half small red onion, quartered
- Three tablespoons of Pete's Western Rub or Poultry Seasoning, divided
- Three celery stalks, chopped into large chunks

For the sauce

- Two cups of orange juice
- Two tablespoons of orange marmalade
- Three teaspoons of grated fresh ginger
- Two tablespoons of soy sauce
- Two tablespoons of honey

Instructions

1. Remove any giblets from the duck's cavity and neck and keep or dispose of them for some purpose. With a paper towel, clean the duck and pat it off.
2. From the tail, spine, and cavity section, trim any extra fat. Using the tip of a sharp paring knife to poke the duck skin all over to make sure that it does not reach the duck meat to promote the removal of the fat layer under the flesh.
3. With one tablespoon of rub or seasoning, season the interior of the cavity.
4. With the remaining rub or seasoning, season the outside of the duck.
5. Stuff the space with orange wedges, celery, and onion. To aid hold the stuffing in, bind the duck legs together with butcher's twine. On a small rack in a shallow roasting pan, put the duck breast-side up.

6. Mix the ingredients in a saucepan over low heat to create the sauce and boil until the sauce thickens and is syrupy.

7. Enable to cool and put aside.

8. Set up your wood pellet smoker-grill for indirect cooking and use some pellets to preheat it to 350 ° F.

9. Roast the duck for 2 hours at 350°F.

10. Brush the duck liberally with the orange sauce after 2 hours.

11. Roast the orange-glazed duck for another 30 minutes and check that the internal temperature exceeds 165 °F at the thickest section of the legs.

12. Until cooking, rest the duck under a loose foil tent for 20 minutes.

13. Throw out the orange wedges, onion and celery. Quarter the duck with shears of poultry and serve.

5.10 Peteizza Meatloaf

Ready in about 3 hours 30 minutes | Servings-8 | Difficulty-Hard

Ingredients

For meatloaf

- Two large eggs
- One cup of Italian bread crumbs
- Half teaspoon of seasoned salt
- One pound pork sausage
- One pound ground beef
- Half teaspoon of garlic salt
- Half teaspoon of ground pepper
- Half teaspoon of granulated garlic

- Half cup of pizza sauce, plus an additional half cup for serving

For stuffing

- Two tablespoons of extra-virgin olive oil
- 2/3 cup of sliced green bell pepper
- A pinch of salt and black pepper
- Three ounces of sliced pepperoni sausage
- One cup of sliced portobello mushrooms
- 2/3 cup of sliced red onion
- Half cup of sliced red bell pepper
- Two cups of shredded mozzarella cheese
- Two cups of shredded cheddar or Jack cheese

Instructions

1. Combine the meatloaf components thoroughly with your hands in a wide bowl to achieve maximum performance.
2. Heat the olive oil over medium-high heat in a medium skillet and sauté the mushrooms, green bell pepper, red onion and red bell pepper until the vegetables are al dente for about 2 minutes. With a pinch of salt and black pepper, season the vegetables. Then set it aside.
3. Flatten the meatloaf into a 3/8-inch-thick rectangle on parchment paper. Range the sautéed vegetables thinly over the meat. Cover the mozzarella with the veggies, accompanied by the cheddar or Jack. Cover the pepperoni with the cheese.
4. Using the parchment paper to roll the meatloaf, ensuring the ends and all seams are covered.

5. Set up your wood pellet-smoker grill for indirect heat and use oak pellets or a mix to preheat it to 225 ° F.

6. Smoke a meatloaf with stuffed pizza for 1 hour.

7. Increase the pit temperature to 350 °F after an hour, and cook until the stuffed pizza meatloaf's internal temperature exceeds 170 °F.

8. Cover the meatloaf with the leftover half cup of pizza sauce and allow to stand for 15 minutes under a loose foiled tent before eating.

5.11 Shrimp-Stuffed Tilapia

Ready in about 1 hour 10 minutes | Servings-5 | Difficulty-Moderate

Ingredients

- Two tablespoons of extra-virgin olive oil
- One and a half teaspoons of Seafood Seasoning or Old Bay seasoning
- Five (four to six-ounce) fresh farmed tilapia fillets
- One and a half teaspoons of smoked paprika

For the shrimp Stuffing

- One tablespoon of salted butter
- One cup of Italian bread crumbs
- One large egg, beaten
- One and a half teaspoons of Fagundes Famous Seasoning or salt and pepper
- One pound of cooked, peeled, deveined, tail-off shrimp
- One cup of finely diced red onion
- Half cup of mayonnaise
- Two teaspoons of fresh chopped parsley or dried parsley

Instructions

1. Get the shrimp stuffing packed. To cut the shrimp finely, use a food processor, salsa maker, or knife.
2. Melt the butter and sauté the red onion in a small skillet over medium-high heat until it is translucent around 3 minutes. Put aside to let the room temperature cool.
3. In a wide cup, mix the shrimp, the cooled sautéed onion and the remaining ingredients.
4. Cover the shrimp stuffing and refrigerate it before ready to use. Shrimp stuffing can be used within two days.
5. With olive oil, rub all sides of the fillets.
6. On the backside of each filet, spoon 1⁄3 cup of the stuffing. Reddish stripping is on the backside of the tilapia fillet.
7. On the lower half of the fillet, flatten out the stuffing. Fold the tilapia in half and make careful to keep the fish in place with two or more toothpicks.
8. With the smoked paprika and seafood seasoning or Old Bay seasoning, dust each fillet.
9. Configure your wood pellet smoker-grill for indirect cooking and use any pellets to preheat it to 400 °F.
10. On a nonstick grilling tray, position the stuffed fillets.
11. Bake the tilapia for 30 to 45 minutes, or until the fish quickly flakes and hits an internal temperature of 145°F.
12. Rest the fish for 5 minutes before serving.

5.12 Easy Smoked Chicken Breasts

Ready in about 45 minutes | Servings-4 | Difficulty-Moderate

Ingredients

- One tablespoon of Olive Oil
- Two tablespoons of Turbinado Sugar
- Two tablespoons of Paprika
- One teaspoon of Black Pepper
- Two tablespoons of garlic powder
- Four Skinless Chicken Breasts Large Boneless
- Two tablespoons of Brown sugar
- One teaspoon of Celery Seed
- Two tablespoons of Kosher salt
- One teaspoon of Cayenne Pepper
- Two tablespoons onion powder

Instructions

1. Mix all the dried ingredients together in a tub.
2. On both sides, pat the chicken breasts to dry and drizzle each side with a little olive oil.
3. Sprinkle the rub liberally on top of the chicken breasts. Enable 15 minutes, or up to 30 minutes, to sit in the fridge (place plastic wrap over the top if over 15 minutes of rest time.)

4. Hot a cigarette smoker (use the super smoke on Traeger) with the lid opened for 5 minutes. Increase the heat to 350 degrees and, as it warms up, shut the cover for 15 minutes.
5. Place the chicken on the grill, spiced side down, and season the underside of the chicken liberally. Cook with the lid closed for 12-13 minutes.
6. Switch over the chicken and cook at 165-170 degrees for another 10-12 minutes or until finished.
7. Take the chicken from the grill and lay a cutting board with foil over the end. Prior to slicing, let the chicken rest for 3-5 minutes.

Chapter 1: Air fryer breakfast recipes

104. 1. Air fryer breakfast frittata

Cook time: 20 minutes

Servings: 2 people

Difficulty: Easy

Ingredients:

- 1 pinch of cayenne pepper (not necessary)
- 1 chopped green onion
- Cooking spray
- 2 tbsp. diced red bell pepper
- ¼ pound fully cooked and crumbled breakfast sausages
- 4 lightly beaten eggs
- ½ cup shredded cheddar-Monterey jack cheese blend

Instructions:

1. Combine eggs, bell pepper, cheddar Monterey Jack cheese, sausages, cayenne and onion inside a bowl & blend to combine.

2. The air fryer should be preheated to 360 ° f (180° c). Spray a 6 by 2-inch non-stick cake pan along with a spray used in cooking.

3. Place the mixture of egg in the ready-made cake tray.

4. Cook for 18 - 20 minutes in your air fryer before the frittata is ready.

105. 2. Air fryer banana bread

Cook time: 28 minutes

Serving: 8 people

Difficulty: Easy

Ingredients:

- 3/4 cup flour for all purposes
- 1/4 tbsp. salt
- 1 egg
- 2 mashed bananas overripe
- 1/4 cup sour cream
- 1/2 cup sugar
- 1/4 tbsp. baking soda
- 7-inch bundt pan

- 1/4 cup vegetable oil
- 1/2 tbsp. vanilla

Instructions:

1. In one tub, combine the dry ingredients and the wet ones in another. Mix the two slowly till flour is fully integrated, don't over mix.

2. With an anti-stick spray, spray and on a 7-inch bundt pan & then pour in the bowl.

3. Put it inside the air fryer basket & close. Placed it for 28 mins to 310 degrees

4. Remove when completed & permit to rest in the pan for about 5 mins.

5. When completed, detach and allow 5 minutes to sit in the pan. Then flip on a plate gently. Sprinkle melted icing on top, serve after slicing.

106. 3. Easy air fryer omelet

Cook time: 8 minutes

Serving: 2 people

Difficulty: Easy

Ingredients:

- 1/4 cup shredded cheese
- 2 eggs
- Pinch of salt
- 1 teaspoon of McCormick morning breakfast seasoning - garden herb
- Fresh meat & veggies, diced
- 1/4 cup milk

Instructions:

1. In a tiny tub, mix the milk and eggs till all of them are well mixed.
2. Add a little salt in the mixture of an egg.
3. Then, in the mixture of egg, add the veggies.
4. Pour the mixture of egg in a greased pan of 6 by 3 inches.
5. Place your pan inside the air fryer container.
6. Cook for about 8 to 10 mins and at 350 f.
7. While you are cooking, slather the breakfast seasoning over the eggs & slather the cheese on the top.
8. With a thin spoon, loose the omelet from the pan and pass it to a tray.

9. Loosen the omelet from the sides of the pan with a thin spatula and pass it to a tray.

10. Its options to garnish it with additional green onions.

107. 4. Air-fried breakfast bombs

Cook time: 20 mins

Serving: 2

Difficulty: easy

Ingredients:

- Cooking spray
- 1 tbsp. fresh chives chopped
- 3 lightly beaten, large eggs
- 4 ounces whole-wheat pizza dough freshly prepared
- 3 bacon slices center-cut
- 1 ounce 1/3-less-fat softened cream cheese

Instructions:

1. Cook the bacon in a standard size skillet for around 10 minutes, medium to very crisp. Take the bacon out of the pan; scatter. Add the eggs to the bacon drippings inside the pan; then cook, stirring constantly, around 1 minute, until almost firm and yet loose. Place the eggs in a bowl; add the cream cheese, the chives, and the crumbled bacon.

2. Divide the dough into four identical sections. Roll each bit into a five-inch circle on a thinly floured surface. Place a quarter of the egg mixture in the middle of each circle of dough. Clean the underside of the dough with the help of water; wrap the dough all around the mixture of an egg to form a purse and pinch the dough.

3. Put dough purses inside the air fryer basket in one layer; coat really well with the help of cooking spray. Cook for 5 to 6 minutes at 350 degrees f till it turns to a golden brown; check after 4 mins.

108. 5. Air fryer French toast

Cook time: 15 mins

Serving: 2 people

Difficulty: easy

Ingredients:

- 4 beaten eggs
- 4 slices of bread
- Cooking spray (non-stick)

Instructions:

1. Put the eggs inside a container or a bowl which is sufficient and big, so the pieces of bread will fit inside.

2. With a fork, mix the eggs and after that, place each bread slice over the mixture of an egg.

3. Turn the bread for one time so that every side is filled with a mixture of an egg.

4. After that, fold a big sheet of aluminum foil; this will keep the bread together. Switch the foil's side; this will ensure that the mixture of an egg may not get dry. Now put the foil basket in the air fryer basket. Make sure to allow space around the edges; this will let the circulation of hot air.

5. With the help of cooking spray, spray the surface of the foil basket and then put the bread over it. On top, you may add the excess mixture of an egg.

6. For 5 mins, place the time to 365 degrees f.

7. Turn the bread & cook it again for about 3 to 5 mins, until it's golden brown over the top of the French toast & the egg isn't runny.

8. Serve it hot, with toppings of your choice.

109. 6. Breakfast potatoes in the air fryer

Cook time: 15 mins

Servings: 2

Difficulty: easy

Ingredients:

- 1/2 tbsp. kosher salt
- 1/2 tbsp. garlic powder
- Breakfast potato seasoning
- 1/2 tbsp. smoked paprika
- 1 tbsp. oil
- 5 potatoes medium-sized. Peeled & cut to one-inch cubes (Yukon gold works best)
- 1/4 tbsp. black ground pepper

Instructions:

1. At 400 degrees f, preheat the air fryer for around 2 to 3 minutes. Doing this will provide you the potatoes that are crispiest.

2. Besides that, brush your potatoes with oil and breakfast potato seasoning till it is fully coated.

3. Using a spray that's non-stick, spray on the air fryer. Add potatoes & cook for about 15 mins, shaking and stopping the basket for 2 to 3 times so that you can have better cooking.

4. Place it on a plate & serve it immediately.

110. 7. Air fryer breakfast pockets

Cook time: 15 mins

Serving: 5 people

Difficulty: easy

Ingredients:

- 2-gallon zip lock bags
- Salt & pepper to taste

- 1/3 + 1/4 cup of whole milk
- 1 whole egg for egg wash
- Cooking spray
- 1-2 ounces of Velveeta cheese
- Parchment paper
- 1 lb. of ground pork
- 2 packages of Pillsbury pie crust
- 2 crusts to a package
- 4 whole eggs

Instructions:

1. Let the pie crusts out of the freezer.
2. Brown the pig and rinse it.
3. In a tiny pot, heat 1/4 cup of cheese and milk until it is melted.
4. Whisk four eggs, season with pepper and salt & add the rest of the milk.
5. Fumble the eggs in the pan until they are nearly fully cooked.
6. Mix the eggs, cheese and meat together.
7. Roll out the pie crust & cut it into a circle of about 3 to 4 inches (cereal bowl size).
8. Whisk 1 egg for making an egg wash.
9. Put around 2 tbsp. of the blend in the center of every circle.

10. Now, eggs wash the sides of the circle.

11. Create a moon shape by folding the circle.

12. With the help of a fork, folded edges must be crimped

13. Place the pockets inside parchment paper & put it inside a ziplock plastic bag overnight.

14. Preheat the air fryer for 360 degrees until it is ready to serve.

15. With a cooking spray, each pocket side must be sprayed.

16. Put pockets inside the preheated air fryer for around 15 mins or till they are golden brown.

17. Take it out from the air fryer & make sure it's cool before you serve it.

111. 8. Air fryer sausage breakfast casserole

Cook time: 20 mins

Serving: 6 people

Difficulty: easy

Ingredients:

- 1 diced red bell pepper
- 1 lb. ground breakfast sausage
- 4 eggs
- 1 diced green bell pepper

- 1/4 cup diced sweet onion
- 1 diced yellow bell pepper
- 1 lb. hash browns

Instructions:

1. Foil line your air fryer's basket.
2. At the bottom, put some hash browns.
3. Cover it with the raw sausage.
4. Place the onions & peppers uniformly on top.
5. Cook for 10 mins at 355 degrees.
6. Open your air fryer & blend the casserole a little if necessary.
7. Break every egg inside the bowl and spill it directly over the casserole.
8. Cook for the next 10 minutes for 355 degrees.
9. Serve with pepper and salt for taste.

112. 9. Breakfast egg rolls

Cook time: 15 mins

Servings: 6 people

Difficulty: easy

Ingredients:

- Black pepper, to taste
- 6 large eggs
- Olive oil spray
- 2 tbsp. chopped green onions
- 1 tablespoon water
- 1/4 teaspoon kosher salt
- 2 tablespoons diced red bell pepper
- 1/2 pound turkey or chicken sausage
- 12 egg roll wrappers

- The salsa that is optional for dipping

Instructions:

1. Combine the water, salt and black pepper with the eggs.

2. Cook sausage in a non-stick skillet of medium size, make sure to let it cook in medium heat till there's no pink color left for 4 minutes, splitting into crumbles, then drain.

3. Stir in peppers and scallions & cook it for 2 minutes. Put it on a plate.

4. Over moderate flame, heat your skillet & spray it with oil.

5. Pour the egg mixture & cook stirring till the eggs are cooked and fluffy. Mix the sausage mixture.

6. Put one wrapped egg roll on a dry, clean work surface having corners aligned like it's a diamond.

7. Include an egg mixture of 1/4 cup on the lower third of your wrapper.

8. Gently raise the lower point closest to you & tie it around your filling.

9. Fold the right & left corners towards the middle & continue rolling into the compact cylinder.

10. Do this again with the leftover wrappers and fillings.

11. Spray oil on every side of your egg roll & rub it with hands to cover them evenly.

12. The air fryer must be preheated to 370 degrees f.

13. Cook the egg rolls for about 10 minutes in batches till it's crispy and golden brown.

14. Serve instantly with salsa, if required.

113. 10. Air fryer breakfast casserole

Cook time: 45 mins

Servings: 6 people

Difficulty: medium

Ingredients:

- 1 tbsp. extra virgin olive oil
- Salt and pepper
- 4 bacon rashers
- 1 tbsp. oregano
- 1 tbsp. garlic powder
- 2 bread rolls stale
- 1 tbsp. parsley
- 320 grams grated cheese
- 4 sweet potatoes of medium size
- 3 spring onions
- 8 pork sausages of medium size
- 11 large eggs
- 1 bell pepper

Instructions:

1. Dice and peel the sweet potato in cubes. Mix the garlic, salt, oregano and pepper in a bowl with olive oil of extra virgin.

2. In an air fryer, put your sweet potatoes. Dice the mixed peppers, cut the sausages in quarters & dice the bacon.

3. Add the peppers, bacon and sausages over the sweet potatoes. Air fry it at 160c or 320 f for 15 mins.

4. Cube and slice the bread when your air fryer is heating & pound your eggs in a blending jug with the eggs, including some extra parsley along with pepper and salt. Dice the spring onion.

5. Check the potatoes when you hear a beep from the air fryer. A fork is needed to check on the potatoes. If you are unable to, then cook for a further 2 to 3 minutes. Mix the basket of the air fryer, include the spring onions & then cook it for an additional five minutes with the same temperature and cooking time.

6. Using the projected baking pans, place the components of your air fryer on 2 of them. Mix it while adding bread and cheese. Add your mixture of egg on them & they are primed for the actual air fry.

7. Put the baking pan inside your air fryer & cook for 25 minutes for 160 c or 320 f. If you planned to cook 2, cook 1 first and then the other one. Place a cocktail stick into the middle & then it's done if it comes out clear and clean.

114. 11. Air fryer breakfast sausage ingredients

Cook time: 10 mins

Serving: 2 people

Difficulty: easy

Ingredients:

- 1 pound breakfast sausage
- Air fryer breakfast sausage ingredients

Instructions:

1. Insert your sausage links in the basket of an air fryer.
2. Cook your sausages or the sausage links for around 8 to 10 minutes at 360°.

115. 12. Wake up air fryer avocado boats

Cook time: 5 mins

Servings: 2

Difficulty: easy

Ingredients:

- 1/2 teaspoon salt
- 2 plum tomatoes, seeded & diced
- 1/4 teaspoon black pepper
- 1 tablespoon finely diced jalapeno (optional)
- 4 eggs (medium or large recommended)
- 1/4 cup diced red onion
- 2 avocados, halved & pitted
- 1 tablespoon lime juice
- 2 tablespoons chopped fresh cilantro

Instructions:

1. Squeeze the avocado fruit out from the skin with a spoon, leaving the shell preserved. Dice the avocado and put it in a bowl of medium-sized. Combine it with onion, jalapeno (if there is a need), tomato, pepper and cilantro. Refrigerate and cover the mixture of avocado until ready for usage.

2. Preheat the air-fryer for 350° f

3. Place the avocado shells on a ring made up of failing to make sure they don't rock when cooking. Just roll 2 three-inch-wide strips of aluminum foil into rope shapes to create them, and turn each one into a three-inch circle. In an air fryer basket, put every avocado shell over a foil frame. Break an egg in every avocado shell & air fry for 5 - 7 minutes or when needed.

4. Take it out from the basket; fill including avocado salsa & serve.

116. 12. Air fryer cinnamon rolls

Cook time: 15 mins

Serving: 2 people

Difficulty: easy

Ingredients:

- 1 spray must non-stick cooking spray
- 1 can cinnamon rolls we used Pillsbury

Instructions:

1. put your cinnamon rolls inside your air fryer's basket, with the help of the rounds of 2. Parchment paper or by the cooking spray that is non-stick.
2. Cook at around 340 degrees f, 171 degrees for about 12 to 15 minutes, for one time.
3. Drizzle it with icing, place it on a plate and then serve.

117. 13. Air-fryer all-American breakfast dumplings

Cook: 10 minutes

Servings: 1 person

Difficulty: easy

Ingredients:

- Dash salt
- 1/2 cup (about four large) egg whites or liquid egg fat-free substitute
- 1 tbsp. Pre-cooked real crumbled bacon
- 1 wedge the laughing cow light creamy Swiss cheese (or 1 tbsp. reduced-fat cream cheese)

- 8 wonton wrappers or gyoza

Instructions:

1. By using a non-stick spray, spray your microwave-safe bowl or mug. Include egg whites or any substitute, salt and cheese wedge. Microwave it for around 1.5 minutes, mixing in between until cheese gets well mixed and melted and the egg is set.

2. Mix the bacon in. Let it cool completely for about 5 minutes.

3. Cover a wrapper of gyoza with the mixture of an egg (1 tablespoon). Moist the corners with water & fold it in half, having the filling. Tightly push the corners to seal. Repeat this step to make seven more dumplings. Make sure to use a non-stick spray for spraying.

4. Insert the dumplings inside your air fryer in one single layer. (Save the leftover for another round if they all can't fit). Adjust the temperature to 375 or the closest degree. Cook it for around 5 mins or till it's crispy and golden brown.

Chapter 2: Air fryer seafood recipe

118. 1. Air fryer 'shrimp boil'

Cook time: 15 mins

Servings: 2 people

Difficulty: easy

Ingredients:

- 2 tbsp. vegetable oil
- 1 lb. easy-peel defrosted shrimp
- 3 small red potatoes cut 1/2 inch rounds
- 1 tbsp. old bay seasoning
- 2 ears of corn cut into thirds
- 14 oz. smoked sausage, cut into three-inch pieces

Instructions:

1. Mix all the items altogether inside a huge tub & drizzle it with old bay seasoning, peppers, oil and salt. Switch to the air fryer basket attachment & place the basket over the pot.

2. Put inside your air fryer & adjust the setting of fish; make sure to flip after seven minutes.

3. Cautiously remove & then serve.

119. 2. Air fryer fish & chips

Cook time: 10 mins

Serving: 6 people

Difficulty: easy

Ingredients:

- Tartar sauce for serving
- ½ tbsp. garlic powder
- 1 pound cod fillet cut into strips
- Black pepper
- 2 cups panko breadcrumbs
- ½ cup all-purpose flour
- ¼ tbsp. salt
- Large egg beaten
- Lemon wedges for serving
- 2 teaspoons paprika

Instructions:

1. In a tiny tub, combine the flour, adding salt, paprika and garlic powder. Put your beaten egg in one bowl & your panko breadcrumbs in another bowl.

2. Wipe your fish dry with a towel. Dredge your fish with the mixture of flour, now the egg & gradually your panko breadcrumbs, pushing down gently till your crumbs stick. Spray both ends with oil.

3. Fry at 400 degrees f. Now turn halfway for around 10 to 12 mins until it's lightly brown and crispy.

4. Open your basket & search for preferred crispiness with the help of a fork to know if it easily flakes off. You may hold fish for an extra 1 to 2 mins as required.

5. Serve instantly with tartar sauce and fries, if required.

120. 3. Air-fryer scallops

Cook time: 20 mins

Servings: 2 people

Difficulty: easy

Ingredients:

- ¼ cup extra-virgin olive oil
- ½ tbsp. garlic finely chopped
- Cooking spray
- ½ teaspoons finely chopped garlic
- 8 large (1-oz.) Sea scallops, cleaned & patted very dry

- 1 tbsp. finely grated lemon zest
- ⅛ tbsp. salt
- 2 tbsps. Very finely chopped flat-leaf parsley
- 2 tbsp. capers, very finely chopped
- ¼ tbsp. ground pepper

Instructions:

1. Sprinkle the scallops with salt and pepper. Cover the air fryer basket by the cooking spray. Put your scallops inside the basket & cover them by the cooking spray. Put your basket inside the air fryer. Cook your scallops at a degree of 400 f till they attain the temperature of about 120 degrees f, which is an international temperature for 6 mins.

2. Mix capers, oil, garlic, lemon zest and parsley inside a tiny tub. Sprinkle over your scallops.

121. 4. Air fryer tilapia

Cook time: 6 mins

Servings: 4 people

Difficulty: easy

Ingredients:

- 1/2 tbsp. paprika
- 1 tbsp. salt
- 2 eggs

- 4 fillets of tilapia
- 1 tbsp. garlic powder
- 1/2 teaspoon black pepper
- 1/2 cup flour
- 2 tbsp. lemon zest
- 1 tbsp. garlic powder
- 4 ounces parmesan cheese, grated

Instructions:

1. Cover your tilapia fillets:

Arrange three deep dishes. Out of these, put flour in one. Blend egg in second and make sure that the eggs are whisked in the last dish mix lemon zest, cheese, pepper, paprika and salt. Ensure that the tilapia fillets are dry, and after that dip, every fillet inside the flour & covers every side. Dip into your egg wash & pass them for coating every side of the fillet to your cheese mixture.

2. Cook your tilapia:

Put a tiny sheet of parchment paper in your bask of air fryer and put 1 - 2 fillets inside the baskets. Cook at 400°f for around 4 - 5 minutes till the crust seems golden brown, and the cheese completely melts.

122. 5. Air fryer salmon

Cook time: 7 mins

Serving: 2 people

Difficulty: easy

Ingredients:

- 1/2 tbsp. salt
- 2 tbsp. olive oil
- 1/4 teaspoon ground black pepper

- 2 salmon fillets (about 1 1/2-inches thick)
- 1/2 teaspoon ginger powder
- 2 teaspoons smoked paprika
- 1 teaspoon onion powder
- 1/4 teaspoon red pepper flakes
- 1 tbsp. garlic powder
- 1 tablespoon brown sugar (optional)

Instructions:

1. Take the fish out of the refrigerator, check if there are any bones, & let it rest for 1 hour on the table.

2. Combine all the ingredients in a tub.

3. Apply olive oil in every fillet & then the dry rub solution.

4. Put the fillets in the Air Fryer basket.

5. set the air fryer for 7 minutes at the degree of 390 if your fillets have a thickness of 1-1/2-inches.

6. As soon as the timer stops, test fillets with a fork's help to ensure that they are ready to the perfect density. If you see that there is any need, then you cook it for a further few minutes. Your cooking time may vary with the temperature & size of the fish. It is best to set your air fryer for a minimum time, and then you may increase the time if there is a need. This will prevent the fish from being overcooked.

123. 6. Blackened fish tacos in the air fryer

Cook time: 9 mins

Serving: 4 people

Difficulty: easy

Ingredients:

- 1 lb. Mahi mahi fillets (can use cod, catfish, tilapia or salmon)
- Cajun spices blend (or use 2-2.5 tbsp. store-bought Cajun spice blend)
- ¾ teaspoon salt
- 1 tbsp. paprika (regular, not smoked)
- 1 teaspoon oregano
- ½-¾ teaspoon cayenne (reduces or skips to preference)
- ½ teaspoon garlic powder

- ½ teaspoon onion powder
- ½ teaspoon black pepper
- 1 teaspoon brown sugar (skip for low-carb)

Additional ingredients for tacos:

- Mango salsa
- Shredded cabbage (optional)
- 8 corn tortillas

Instructions:

1. Get the fish ready

2. Mix cayenne, onion powder, brown sugar, salt, oregano, garlic powder, paprika and black pepper in a deep mixing tub.

3. Make sure to get the fish dry by using paper towels. Drizzle or brush the fish with a little amount of any cooking oil or olive oil. This allows the spices to stick to the fish.

4. Sprinkle your spice mix graciously on a single edge of your fish fillets. Rub the fish softly, so the ingredients stay on the fish.

5. Flip and brush the fish with oil on the other side & sprinkle with the leftover spices. Press the ingredients inside the fish softly.

6. Turn the air fryer on. Inside the basket put your fish fillets. Do not overlap the pan or overfill it. Close your basket.

7. Air fry the fish

8. Set your air fryer for 9 mins at 360°f. If you are using fillets which are thicker than an inch, then you must increase the cooking time to ten minutes. When the air fryer timer stops, with the help of a fish spatula or long tongs, remove your fish fillets.

9. Assembling the tacos

10. Heat the corn tortillas according to your preference. Conversely, roll them inside the towel made up of wet paper & heat them in the microwave for around 20 to 30 seconds.

11. Stack 2 small fillets or insert your fish fillet. Add a few tablespoons of your favorite mango salsa or condiment & cherish the scorched fish tacos.

12. Alternatively, one can include a few cabbages shredded inside the tacos & now add fish fillets on the top.

124. 7. Air fryer cod

Cook time: 16 mins

Servings: 2 people

Difficulty: easy

Ingredients:

- 2 teaspoon of light oil for spraying
- 1 cup of plantain flour
- 0.25 teaspoon of salt
- 12 pieces of cod about 1 ½ pound
- 1 teaspoon of garlic powder
- 0.5 cup gluten-free flour blend
- 2 teaspoon of smoked paprika
- 4 teaspoons of Cajun seasoning or old bay
- Pepper to taste

Instructions:

1. Spray some oil on your air fryer basket & heat it up to 360° f.

2. Combine the ingredients in a tub & whisk them to blend. From your package, take the cod out and, with the help of a paper towel, pat dry.

3. Dunk every fish piece in the mixture of flour spice and flip it over & push down so that your fish can be coated.

4. Get the fish inside the basket of your air fryer. Ensure that there is room around every fish piece so that the air can flow round the fish.

5. Cook for around 8 minutes & open your air fryer so that you can flip your fish. Now cook another end for around 8 mins.

6. Now cherish the hot serving with lemon.

125. 8. Air fryer miso-glazed Chilean sea bass

Cook time: 20 mins

Serving: 2 people

Difficulty: easy

Ingredients:

- 1/2 teaspoon ginger paste
- Fresh cracked pepper
- 1 tbsp. unsalted butter
- Olive oil for cooking
- 1 tbsp. rice wine vinegar
- 2 tbsp. miring
- 1/4 cup white miso paste

- 2 6 ounce Chilean sea bass fillets
- 4 tbsp. Maple syrup, honey works too.

Instructions:

1. Heat your air fryer to 375 degrees f. Apply olive oil onto every fish fillet and complete it with fresh pepper. Sprat olive oil on the pan of the air fryer and put the skin of the fish. Cook for about 12 to 15 minutes till you see the upper part change into golden brown color & the inner temperature now reached 135-degree f.

2. When the fish is getting cooked, you must have the butter melted inside a tiny saucepan in medium heat. When you notice that the butter melts, add maple syrup, ginger paste, miso paste, miring and rice wine vinegar, mix all of them till they are completely combined, boil them in a light flame and take the pan out instantly from the heat.

3. When your fish is completely done, brush the glaze and fish sides with the help of silicone pastry. Put it back inside your air fryer for around 1 to 2 extra minutes at 375 degrees f, till the glaze is caramelized. Complete it with green onion (sliced) & sesame seeds.

Instructions for oven

1. Heat the oven around 425 degrees f and put your baking sheet and foil sprayed with light olive oil. Bake it for about 20 to 25 minutes; this depends on how thick the fish is. The inner temperature must be around 130 degrees f when your fish is completely cooked.

2. Take out your fish, placed it in the oven & heat the broiler on a high flame. Now the fish must be brushed with miso glaze from the sides and the top & then put the fish inside the oven in the above rack. If the rack is very much near with your broiler, then place it a bit down, you might not want the fish to touch the broiler. Cook your fish for around 1 to 2 minutes above the broiler till you see it's getting caramelize. Make sure to keep a check on it as it happens very quickly. Complete it with the help of green onions (sliced) and sesame seeds.

126. 9. Air fryer fish tacos

Cook time: 35 mins

Serving: 6 people

Difficulty: Medium

Ingredients:

- ¼ teaspoon salt
- ¼ cup thinly sliced red onion
- 1 tbsp. water
- 2 tbsp. sour cream
- Sliced avocado, thinly sliced radishes, chopped fresh cilantro leaves and lime wedges
- 1 teaspoon lime juice
- ½ lb. skinless white fish fillets (such as halibut or mahi-mahi), cut into 1-inch strips
- 1 tbsp. mayonnaise
- 1 egg
- 1 package (12 bowls) old el Paso mini flour tortilla taco bowls, heated as directed on package
- 1 clove garlic, finely chopped
- ½ cup Progresso plain panko crispy bread crumbs
- 1 ½ cups shredded green cabbage
- 2 tbsp. old el Paso original taco seasoning mix (from 1-oz package)

Instructions:

1. Combine the sour cream, garlic, salt, mayonnaise and lime juice together in a medium pot. Add red onion and cabbage; flip to coat. Refrigerate and cover the mixture of cabbage until fit for serving.

2. Cut an 8-inch circle of parchment paper for frying. Place the basket at the bottom of the air fryer.

3. Place the taco-seasoning mix in a deep bowl. Beat the egg & water in another small bowl. Place the bread crumbs in another shallow dish. Coat the fish with your taco seasoning mix; dip inside the beaten egg, then cover with the mixture of bread crumbs, pressing to hold to it.

127. 10. Air fryer southern fried catfish

Cook time: 13 mins

Servings: 4 people

Difficulty: easy

Ingredients:

- 1 lemon
- 1/4 teaspoon cayenne pepper
- Cornmeal seasoning mix
- 1/4 teaspoon granulated onion powder
- 1/2 cup cornmeal
- 1/2 teaspoon kosher salt
- 1/4 teaspoon chili powder
- 2 pounds catfish fillets
- 1/4 teaspoon garlic powder
- 1 cup milk
- 1/4 cup all-purpose flour
- 1/4 teaspoon freshly ground black pepper
- 2 tbsp. dried parsley flakes
- 1/2 cup yellow mustard

Instructions:

1. Add milk and put the catfish in a flat dish.

2. Slice the lemon in two & squeeze around two tbsp. of juice added into milk so that the buttermilk can be made.

3. Place the dish in the refrigerator & leave it for 15 minutes to soak the fillets.

4. Combine the cornmeal-seasoning mixture in a small bowl.

5. Take the fillets out from the buttermilk & pat them dry with the help of paper towels.

6. Spread the mustard evenly on both sides of the fillets.

7. Dip every fillet into a mixture of cornmeal & coat well to create a dense coating.

8. Place the fillets in the greased basket of the air fryer. Spray gently with olive oil.

9. Cook for around 10 minutes at 390 to 400 degrees. Turn over the fillets & spray them with oil & cook for another 3 to 5 mins.

128. 11. Air fryer lobster tails with lemon butter

Cook time: 8 mins

Serving: 2 people

Difficulty: easy

Ingredients:

- 1 tbsp. fresh lemon juice
- 2 till 6 oz. Lobster tails, thawed
- Fresh chopped parsley for garnish (optional)
- 4 tbsp. melted salted butter

Instructions:

1. Make lemon butter combining lemon and melted butter. Mix properly & set aside.

2. Wash lobster tails & absorb the water with a paper towel. Butter your lobster tails by breaking the shell, take out the meat & place it over the shell.

3. Preheat the air fryer for around 5 minutes to 380 degrees. Place the ready lobster tails inside the basket of air fryer, drizzle with single tbsp. melted lemon butter on the meat of lobster. Cover the basket of the air fryer and cook for around 8 minutes at 380 degrees f, or when the lobster meat is not translucent. Open the air fryer halfway into the baking time, and then drizzle with extra lemon butter. Continue to bake until finished.

4. Remove the lobster tails carefully, garnish with crushed parsley if you want to, & plate. For dipping, serve with additional lemon butter.

129. 12. Air fryer crab cakes with spicy aioli + lemon vinaigrette

Cook time: 20 mins

Servings: 2 people

Difficulty: easy

Ingredients:

For the crab cakes:

- 1. Avocado oil spray
- 16-ounce lump crab meat
- 1 egg, lightly beaten
- 2 tbsp. finely chopped red or orange pepper
- 1 tbsp. Dijon mustard
- 2 tbsp. finely chopped green onion
- 1/4 teaspoon ground pepper
- 1/4 cup panko breadcrumbs
- 2 tbsp. olive oil mayonnaise

For the aioli:

- 1/4 teaspoon cayenne pepper
- 1/4 cup olive oil mayonnaise
- 1 teaspoon white wine vinegar
- 1 teaspoon minced shallots

- 1 teaspoon Dijon mustard

For the vinaigrette:

- 2 tbsp. extra virgin olive oil
- 1 tbsp. white wine vinegar
- 4 tbsp. fresh lemon juice, about 1 ½ lemon
- 1 teaspoon honey
- 1 teaspoon lemon zest

To serve:

- Balsamic glaze, to taste
- 2 cups of baby arugula

Instructions:

1. Make your crab cake. Mix red pepper, mayonnaise, ground pepper, crab meat, onion, panko and Dijon in a huge bowl. Make sure to mix the ingredients well. Then add eggs & mix the mixture again till it's mixed well. Take around 1/4 cup of the mixture of crab into cakes which are around 1 inch thick. Spray with avocado oil gently.

2. Cook your crab cakes. Organize crab cakes in one layer in the air fryer. It depends on the air fryer how many batches will be required to cook them. Cook for 10 minutes at 375 degrees f. Take it out from your air fryer & keep it warm. Do this again if required.

3. Make aioli. Combine shallots, Dijon, vinegar, cayenne pepper and mayo. Put aside for serving until ready.

4. Make the vinaigrette. Combine honey, white vinegar, and lemon zest and lemon juice in a ting jar. Include olive oil & mix it well until mixed together.

5. Now serve. Split your arugula into 2 plates. Garnish with crab cakes. Drizzle it with vinaigrette & aioli. Include few drizzles of balsamic glaze if desired.

Chapter 3: Air Fryer Meat and Beef recipe

130. 1. Air fryer steak

Cook time: 35 mins

Servings: 2

Difficulty: Medium

Ingredients:

- Freshly ground black pepper
- 1 tsp. freshly chopped chives
- 2 cloves garlic, minced
- 1(2 lb.) Bone-in rib eye
- 4 tbsp. Butter softened
- 1 tsp. Rosemary freshly chopped
- 2 tsp. Parsley freshly chopped
- 1 tsp. Thyme freshly chopped
- Kosher salt

Instructions:

1. In a tiny bowl, mix herbs and butter. Put a small layer of the wrap made up of plastic & roll in a log. Twist the ends altogether to make it refrigerate and tight till it gets hardened for around 20 minutes.

2. Season the steak with pepper and salt on every side.

3. Put the steak in the air-fryer basket & cook it around 400 degrees for 12 - 14 minutes, in medium temperature, depending on the thickness of the steak, tossing half-way through.

4. Cover your steak with the herb butter slice to serve.

131. 2. Air-fryer ground beef wellington

Cook time: 20 mins

Serving: 2 people

Difficulty: easy

Ingredients:

- 1 large egg yolk
- 1 tsp. dried parsley flakes
- 2 tsp. flour for all-purpose
- 1/2 cup fresh mushrooms chopped
- 1 tbsp. butter
- 1/2 pound of ground beef
- 1 lightly beaten, large egg, it's optional
- 1/4 tsp. of pepper, divided
- 1/4 tsp. of salt
- 1 tube (having 4 ounces) crescent rolls refrigerated
- 2 tbsp. onion finely chopped

• 1/2 cup of half & half cream

Instructions:

1. Preheat the fryer to 300 degrees. Heat the butter over a moderate flame in a saucepan. Include mushrooms; stir, and cook for 5-6 minutes, until tender. Add flour & 1/8 of a tsp. of pepper when mixed. Add cream steadily. Boil it; stir and cook until thickened, for about 2 minutes. Take it out from heat & make it aside.

2. Combine 2 tbsp. of mushroom sauce, 1/8 tsp. of the remaining pepper, onion and egg yolk in a tub. Crumble over the mixture of beef and blend properly. Shape it into two loaves. Unroll and divide the crescent dough into two rectangles; push the perforations to close. Put meatloaf over every rectangle. Bring together the sides and press to seal. Brush it with one beaten egg if necessary.

3. Place the wellingtons on the greased tray inside the basket of the air fryer in a single sheet. Cook till see the thermometer placed into the meatloaf measures 160 degrees, 18 to 22 minutes and until you see golden brown color.

Meanwhile, under low pressure, warm the leftover sauce; mix in the parsley. Serve your sauce, adding wellington.

132. 3. Air-fried burgers

Cook time: 10 mins

Serving: 4 people

Difficulty: easy

Ingredients:

• 500 g of raw ground beef (1 lb.)

- 1 tsp. of Maggi seasoning sauce
- 1/2 tsp. of ground black pepper
- 1 tsp. parsley (dried)
- Liquid smoke (some drops)
- 1/2 tsp. of salt (salt sub)
- 1 tbsp. of Worcestershire sauce
- 1/2 tsp. of onion powder
- 1/2 tsp. of garlic powder

Instructions:

1. Spray the above tray, and set it aside. You don't have to spray your basket if you are having an air fryer of basket-type. The cooking temperature for basket types will be around 180 c or 350 f.

2. Mix all the spice things together in a little tub, such as the sauce of Worcestershire and dried parsley.

2. In a huge bowl, add it inside the beef.

3. Mix properly, and make sure to overburden the meat as this contributes to hard burgers.

4. Divide the mixture of beef into four, & the patties are to be shape off. Place your indent in the middle with the thumb to keep the patties from scrunching up on the center.

5. Place tray in the air fry; gently spray the surfaces of patties.

6. Cook for around 10 minutes over medium heat (or more than that to see that your food is complete). You don't have to turn your patties.

7. Serve it hot on a pan with your array of side dishes.

133. 4. Air fryer meatloaf

Cook time: 25 mins

Serving: 4 people

Difficulty: easy

Ingredients:

- 1/2 tsp. of Salt
- 1 tsp. of Worcestershire sauce
- 1/2 finely chopped, small onion
- 1 tbsp. of Yellow mustard
- 2 tbsp. of ketchup, divided
- 1 lb. Lean ground beef
- 1/2 tsp. Garlic powder

- 1/4 cup of dry breadcrumbs
- 1 egg, lightly beaten
- 1/4 tsp. Pepper
- 1 tsp. Italian seasoning

Instructions:

1. Put the onion, 1 tbsp. Ketchup, garlic powder, pepper, ground beef, egg, salt, breadcrumbs, Italian seasoning and Worcestershire sauce in a huge bowl.

2. Use hands to blend your spices with the meat equally, be careful you don't over-mix as it would make it difficult to over mix.

3. Shape meat having two inches height of 4 by 6, loaf. Switch your air fryer to a degree of 370 f & Put that loaf inside your air fryer.

4. Cook for fifteen min at a degree of 370 f.

5. In the meantime, mix the leftover 1 tbsp. of ketchup & the mustard in a tiny bowl.

6. Take the meatloaf out of the oven & spread the mixture of mustard over it.

7. Return the meatloaf to your air fryer & begin to bake at a degree of 370 degrees f till the thermometer placed inside the loaf measures 160 degrees f, around 8 to 10 further minutes.

8. Remove the basket from your air fryer when the meatloaf has touched 160 degrees f & then make the loaf stay inside the air fryer basket for around 5 to 10 minutes, after that slice your meatloaf.

134. 5. Air fryer hamburgers

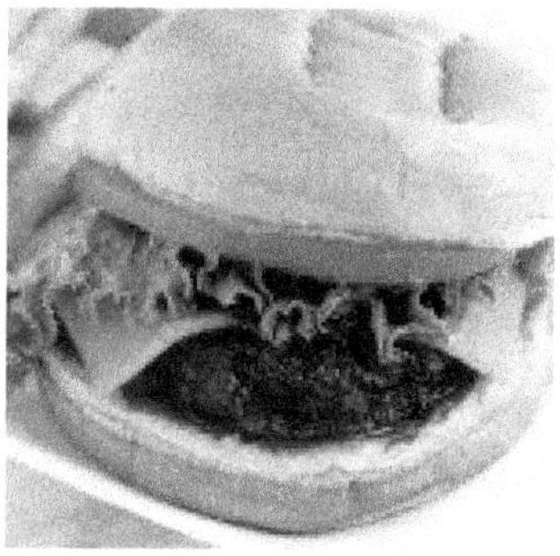

Cook time: 16 mins

Serving: 4 people

Difficulty: easy

Ingredients:

- 1 tsp. of onion powder
- 1 pound of ground beef (we are using 85/15)
- 4 pieces burger buns
- 1 tsp. salt
- 1/4 tsp. of black pepper
- 1 tsp. of garlic powder
- 1 tsp. of Worcestershire sauce

Instructions:

1. Method for standard ground beef:
2. Your air fryer must be preheated to 360 °.
3. In a bowl, put the unprocessed ground beef & add the seasonings.

4. To incorporate everything, make the of use your hands (or you can use a fork) & then shape the mixture in a ball shape (still inside the bowl).

5. Score the mixture of ground beef into 4 equal portions by having a + mark to split it.

Scoop out and turn each segment into a patty.

6. Place it in the air fryer, ensuring each patty has plenty of room to cook (make sure not to touch). If required, one can perform this in groups. We've got a bigger (5.8 quart) air fryer, and we did all of ours in a single batch.

7. Cook, turning half-way back, for 16 minutes. (Note: for bigger patties, you may have a need to cook longer.)

Process for Patties (pre-made):

1. In a tiny bowl, mix onion powder, pepper, garlic powder and salt, then stir till well mixed.

2. In a tiny bowl, pour in a few quantities of Worcestershire sauce. You may require A little more than one teaspoon (such as 1.5 tsp.), as some of it will adhere in your pastry brush.

3. Put patties on a tray & spoon or brush on a thin layer of your Worcestershire sauce.

4. Sprinkle with seasoning on every patty, saving 1/2 for another side.

5. With your hand, rub the seasoning to allow it to stick better.

6. Your air fryer should be preheated to 360 ° f.

7. Take out the basket when it's preheated & gently place your patties, seasoned one down, inside the basket.

8. Side 2 of the season, which is facing up the exact way as per above.

9. In an air fryer, put the basket back and cook for around 16 minutes, tossing midway through.

135. 6. Air Fryer Meatloaf

Cook time: 25 mins

Serving: 4 people

Difficulty: Easy

Ingredients:

- Ground black pepper for taste
- 1 tbsp. of olive oil, or as required
- 1 egg, lightly beaten
- 1 tsp. of salt
- 1 pound of lean ground beef
- 1 tbsp. fresh thyme chopped
- 3 tbsp. of dry bread crumbs
- 1 finely chopped, small onion
- 2 thickly sliced mushrooms

Instructions:

1. Preheat your air fryer to a degree of 392 f (200˚C).

2. Mix together egg, onion, salt, ground beef, pepper, bread crumbs and thyme in a tub. 3. Thoroughly knead & mix.

4. Transfer the mixture of beef in your baking pan & smooth out the surface. The mushrooms are to be pressed from the top & coated with the olive oil. Put the pan inside the basket of the air fryer & slide it inside your air fryer.

5. Set the timer of the air fryer for around 25 minutes & roast the meatloaf till it is nicely browned.

6. Make sure that the meatloaf stays for a minimum of 10 minutes, and after that, you can slice and serve.

136. 7. Air Fryer Beef Kabobs

Cook time: 8 mins

Serving: 4 people

Difficulty: Easy

Ingredients:

- 1 big onion in red color or onion which you want
- 1.5 pounds of sirloin steak sliced into one-inch chunks

- 1 large bell pepper of your choice

For the marinade:

- 1 tbsp. of lemon juice
- Pinch of Salt & pepper
- 4 tbsp. of olive oil
- 1/2 tsp. of cumin
- 1/2 tsp. of chili powder
- 2 cloves garlic minced

Ingredients:

1. In a huge bowl, mix the beef & ingredients to marinade till fully mixed. Cover & marinate for around 30 minutes or up to 24 hours inside the fridge.
2. Preheat your air fryer to a degree of 400 f until prepared to cook. Thread the onion, pepper and beef onto skewers.
3. Put skewers inside the air fryer, which is already heated and the air fryer for about 8 to 10 minutes, rotating half-way until the outside is crispy and the inside is tender.

137. 8. Air-Fried Beef and Vegetable Skewers

Cook time: 8 mins

Serving: 2

Difficulty: easy

Ingredients:

- 2 tbs. of olive oil

- 2 tsp. of fresh cilantro chopped
- Kosher salt & freshly black pepper ground
- 1 tiny yellow summer squash, sliced into one inch (of 2.5-cm) pieces
- 1/4 tsp. of ground coriander
- Lemon wedges to serve (optional)
- 1/8 tsp. of red pepper flakes
- 1 garlic clove, minced
- 1/2 tsp. of ground cumin
- 1/2 yellow bell pepper, sliced into one inch (that's 2.5-cm) pieces
- 1/2 red bell pepper, sliced into one inch (that's 2.5-cm) pieces
- 1/2 lb. (that's 250 g) boneless sirloin, sliced into one inch (of 2.5-cm) cubes
- 1 tiny zucchini, sliced into one inch (that's 2.5-cm) pieces
- 1/2 red onion, sliced into one inch (that's 2.5-cm) pieces

Ingredients:

1. Preheat your air fryer at 390 degrees f (199-degree c).

2. In a tiny bowl, mix together one tablespoon of cumin, red pepper flakes and coriander. Sprinkle the mixture of spices generously over the meat.

3. In a tub, mix together zucchini, oil, cilantro, bell peppers, summer squash, cilantro, onion and garlic. Season with black pepper and salt to taste.

4. Tightly thread the vegetables and meat onto the four skewers adding two layers rack of air fryer, rotating the bits and equally splitting them. Put the skewers over the rack & carefully set your rack inside the cooking basket. Put the basket inside the air fryer. Cook, without covering it for around 7 - 8 minutes, till the vegetables are crispy and tender & your meat is having a medium-rare.

5. Move your skewers to a tray, and if you want, you can serve them with delicious lemon wedges.

138. 9. Air fryer taco calzones

Cook time: 10 mins

Serving: 2 people

Difficulty: easy

Ingredients:

- 1 cup of taco meat
- 1 tube of Pillsbury pizza dough thinly crust
- 1 cup of shredded cheddar

Instructions:

1. Spread out the layer of your pizza dough over a clean table. Slice the dough into four squares with the help of a pizza cutter.

2. By the use of a pizza cutter, cut every square into a big circle. Place the dough pieces aside to create chunks of sugary cinnamon.

3. Cover 1/2 of every dough circle with around 1/4 cup of taco meat & 1/4 cup of shredded cheese.

4. To seal it firmly, fold the remaining over the cheese and meat and push the sides of your dough along with the help of a fork so that it can be tightly sealed. Repeat for all 4 calzones.

5. Each calzone much is gently picked up & spray with olive oil or pan spray. Organize them inside the basket of Air Fryer.

Cook your calzones at a degree of 325 for almost 8 to 10 minutes. Monitor them carefully when it reaches to 8 min mark. This is done so that there is no chance of overcooking.

6. Using salsa & sour cream to serve.

7. For the making of cinnamon sugary chunks, split the dough pieces into pieces having equal sides of around 2 inches long. Put them inside the basket of the air fryer & cook it at a degree of 325 for around 5 minutes. Instantly mix with the one ratio four sugary cinnamon mixtures.

139. 10. Air Fryer Pot Roast

Cook time: 30 mins

Serving: 2 people

Difficulty: Medium

Ingredients:

- 1 tsp. of salt
- 3 tbsp. of brown sugar
- 1/2 cup of orange juice
- 1 tsp. of Worcestershire sauce
- 1/2 tsp. of pepper
- 3–4 pound thawed roast beef chuck roast
- 3 tbsp. of soy sauce

Instructions:

1. Combine brown sugar, Worcestershire sauce, soy sauce and orange juice.

2. Mix till the sugar is completely dissolved.

3. Spillover the roast & marinade for around 8 to 24 hours.

4. Put the roast in the basket of an air fryer.

5. Sprinkle the top with pepper and salt.

6. Air fry it at a degree of 400 f for around 30 minutes, turning it half-way through.

7. Allow it to pause for a period of 3 minutes.

8. Slice and serve into thick cuts.

Chapter 4: midnight snacks

140. 1. Air fryer onion rings

Cook time: 7 mins

Serving: 2 people

Difficulty: easy

Ingredients:

- 2 beaten, large eggs
- Marinara sauce for serving
- 1 ½ tsp. of kosher salt
- ½ tsp. of garlic powder
- 1 medium yellow onion, cut into half in about (1 1/4 cm)
- 1 cup of flour for all-purpose (125 g)
- 1 ½ cups of panko breadcrumbs (172 g)
- 1 tsp. of paprika
- ⅛ tsp. of cayenne
- ½ tsp. of onion powder
- ½ tsp. black pepper freshly ground

Instructions:

1. Preheat your air fryer to 190°c (375°f).

2. Use a medium-size bowl to mix together onion powder, salt, paprika, cayenne, pepper, flour and garlic powder.

3. In 2 separate small cups, add your panko & eggs.

4. Cover onion rings with flour, then with the eggs, and afterward with the panko.

Working in lots, put your onion rings in one layer inside your air fryer & "fry" for 5 to 7 minutes or till you see golden brown color.

5. Using warm marinara sauce to serve.

141. 2. Air fryer sweet potato chips

Cook time: 15 mins

Serving: 2

Difficulty: easy

Ingredients:

- 1 ½ tsp. of kosher salt
- 1 tsp. of dried thyme
- 1 large yam or sweet potato
- ½ tsp. of pepper
- 1 tbsp. of olive oil

Instructions:

1. Preheat your air fryer to a degree of 350 f (180 c).

2. Slice your sweet potato have a length of 3- to 6-mm (1⁄8-1⁄4-inch). In a medium tub, mix your olive oil with slices of sweet potato until well-seasoned. Add some pepper, thyme and salt to cover.

3. Working in groups, add your chips in one sheet & fry for around 14 minutes till you see a golden brown color and slightly crisp.

Fun.

142. 3. Air fryer tortilla chips

Cook time: 5 mins

Serving: 2 people

Difficulty: easy

Ingredients:

- 1 tbsp. of olive oil
- Guacamole for serving
- 2 tsp. of kosher salt
- 12 corn of tortillas
- 1 tbsp. of McCormick delicious jazzy spice blend

Instructions:

1. Preheat your air fryer at a degree of 350 f (180 c).

2. Gently rub your tortillas with olive oil on every side.

3. Sprinkle your tortillas with delicious jazzy spice and salt mix on every side.

Slice every tortilla into six wedges.

4. Functioning in groups, add your tortilla wedges inside your air fryer in one layer & fry it for around 5 minutes or until you see golden brown color and crispy texture.

Serve adding guacamole

143. 4. Air fryer zesty chicken wings

Cook time: 20 mins

Serving: 2 people

Difficulty: easy

Ingredients:

- 1 ½ tsp. of kosher salt
- 1 ½ lb. of patted dry chicken wings (of 680 g)
- 1 tbsp. of the delicious, zesty spice blend

Instructions:

1. Preheat your air fryer at 190°c (375°f).

2. In a tub, get your chicken wings mixed in salt & delicious zesty spice, which must be blend till well-seasoned.

3. Working in lots, add your chicken wings inside the air fryer in one layer & fry it for almost 20 minutes, turning it halfway through.

4. Serve it warm

144. 5. Air fryer sweet potato fries

Cook time: 15 mins

Serving: 2 people

Difficulty: easy

Ingredients:

- 1/4 tsp. of sea salt
- 1 tbsp. of olive oil
- 2 (having 6-oz.) sweet potatoes, cut & peeled into sticks of 1/4-inch
- Cooking spray
- 1/4 tsp. of garlic powder
- 1 tsp. fresh thyme chopped

Instructions:

1. Mix together thyme, garlic powder, olive oil and salt in a bowl. Put sweet potato inside the mixture and mix well to cover.

2. Coat the basket of the air fryer gently with the help of cooking spray. Place your sweet potatoes in one layer inside the basket & cook in groups at a degree of 400 f until soft inside & finely browned from outside for around 14 minutes, rotating the fries halfway through the cooking process.

145. 6. Air fryer churros with chocolate sauce

Cook time: 30 mins

Serving: 12

Difficulty: easy

Ingredients:

- 1/4 cup, adding 2 tbsp. Unsalted butter that's divided into half-cup (around 2 1/8 oz.)
- 3 tbsp. of heavy cream
- Half cup water
- 4 ounces of bitter and sweet finely chopped baking chocolate
- Flour for All-purpose
- 2 tsp. of ground cinnamon
- 2 large eggs
- 1/4 tsp. of kosher salt
- 2 tbsp. of vanilla kefir
- 1/3 cup of granulated sugar

Instruction:

1. Bring salt, water & 1/4 cup butter and boil it in a tiny saucepan with a medium-high flame. Decrease the heat to around medium-low flame; add flour & mix actively with a spoon made up of wood for around 30 seconds.

2. Stir and cook continuously till the dough is smooth. Do this till you see your dough continues to fall away from the sides of the pan & a film appears on the bottom of the pan after 2 to 3 minutes. Move the dough in a medium-sized bowl. Stir continuously for around 1 minute until slightly cooled. Add one egg from time to time while stirring continuously till you see it gets smoother after every addition. Move the mixture in the piping bag, which is fitted with having star tip of medium size. Chill it for around 30 minutes.

3. Pipe 6 (3" long) bits in one-layer inside a basket of the air fryer. Cook at a degree of 380 f for around 10 minutes. Repeat this step for the leftover dough.

4. Stir the sugar & cinnamon together inside a medium-size bowl. Use 2 tablespoons of melted butter to brush the cooked churros. Cover them with the sugar mixture.

5. Put the cream and chocolate in a tiny, microwaveable tub. Microwave with a high temperature for roughly 30 seconds until molten and flat, stirring every 15 seconds. Mix in kefir.

6. Serve the churros, including chocolate sauce.

146. 7. Whole-wheat pizzas in an air fryer

Cook time: 10 mins

Serving: 2 people

Difficulty: easy

Ingredients:

- 1 small thinly sliced garlic clove
- 1/4 ounce of Parmigiano-Reggiano shaved cheese (1 tbsp.)

- 1 cup of small spinach leaves (around 1 oz.)
- 1/4 cup marinara sauce (lower-sodium)
- 1-ounce part-skim pre-shredded mozzarella cheese (1/4 cup)
- 1 tiny plum tomato, sliced into 8 pieces
- 2 pita rounds of whole-wheat

Instructions:

1. Disperse marinara sauce equally on one side of every pita bread. Cover it each with half of the tomato slices, cheese, spinach leaves and garlic.

2. Put 1 pita in the basket of air-fryer & cook it at a degree of 350 f until the cheese is melted and the pita is crispy. Repeat with the leftover pita.

147. 8. Air-fried corn dog bites

Cook time: 15 mins

Serving: 4 people

Difficulty: easy

Ingredients:

- 2 lightly beaten large eggs
- 2 uncured hot dogs of all-beef
- Cooking spray
- 12 bamboo skewers or craft sticks
- 8 tsp. of yellow mustard

- 1 1/2 cups cornflakes cereal finely crushed
- 1/2 cup (2 1/8 oz.) Flour for All-purpose

Instructions:

1. Split lengthwise every hot dog. Cut every half in three same pieces. Add a bamboo skewer or the craft stick inside the end of every hot dog piece.

2. Put flour in a bowl. Put slightly beaten eggs in another shallow bowl. Put crushed cornflakes inside another shallow bowl. Mix the hot dogs with flour; make sure to shake the surplus. Soak in the egg, helping you in dripping off every excess. Dredge inside the cornflakes crumbs, pushing to stick.

3. Gently coat the basket of the air fryer with your cooking spray. Put around six bites of corn dog inside the basket; spray the surface lightly with the help of cooking spray. Now cook at a degree of 375 f till the coating shows a golden brown color and is crunchy for about 10 minutes, flipping the bites of corn dog halfway in cooking. Do this step with other bites of the corn dog.

4. Put three bites of corn dog with 2 tsp. of mustard on each plate to, and then serve immediately.

148. 9. Crispy veggie quesadillas in an air fryer

Cook time: 20 mins

Serving: 4 people

Difficulty: easy

Instructions:

- Cooking spray

- 1/2 cup refrigerated and drained pico de gallo
- 4 ounces far educing cheddar sharp cheese, shredded (1 cup)
- 1 tbsp. of fresh juice (with 1 lime)
- 4(6-in.) whole-grain Sprouted flour tortillas
- 1/4 tsp. ground cumin
- 2 tbsp. fresh cilantro chopped
- 1 cup red bell pepper sliced
- 1 cup of drained & rinsed black beans canned, no-salt-added
- 1 tsp. of lime zest plus
- 1 cup of sliced zucchini
- 2 ounces of plain 2 percent fat reduced Greek yogurt

Instructions:

1. Put tortillas on the surface of your work. Sprinkle two tbsp. Shredded cheese on the half of every tortilla. Each tortilla must be top with cheese, having a cup of 1/4 each black beans, slices of red pepper equally and zucchini slices. Sprinkle equally with the leftover 1/2 cup of cheese. Fold the tortillas making a shape of a half-moon. Coat quesadillas lightly with the help of cooking spray & protect them with toothpicks.

2. Gently spray the cooking spray on the basket of the air fryer. Cautiously put two quesadillas inside the basket & cook it at a degree of 400 f till the tortillas are of golden brown color & slightly crispy, vegetables get softened, and the cheese if finally melted for around 10 minutes, rotating the quesadillas halfway while cooking. Do this step again with the leftover quesadillas.

3. As the quesadillas are cooking, mix lime zest, cumin, yogurt and lime juice altogether in a small tub. For serving, cut the quesadilla in slices & sprinkle it with cilantro. Serve it with a tablespoon of cumin cream and around 2 tablespoons of pico de gallo.

149. 10. Air-fried curry chickpeas

Cook time: 10 mins

Serving: 4 people

Difficulty: easy

Ingredients:

- 2 tbsp. of curry powder
- Fresh cilantro thinly sliced
- 1(15-oz.) Can chickpeas (like garbanzo beans), rinsed & drained (1 1/2 cups)
- 1/4 tsp. of kosher salt
- 1/2 tbsp. of ground turmeric
- 1/2 tsp. of Aleppo pepper
- 1/4 tsp. of ground coriander
- 2 tbsp. of olive oil
- 1/4 tsp. and 1/8 tsp. of Ground cinnamon
- 2 tbsp. of vinegar (red wine)
- 1/4 tsp. of ground cumin

Instructions:

1. Smash chickpeas softly inside a tub with your hands (don't crush); remove chickpea skins.

2. Apply oil and vinegar to chickpeas, & toss for coating. Add turmeric, cinnamon, cumin, curry powder and coriander; whisk gently so that they can be mixed together.

3. Put chickpeas in one layer inside the bask of air fryer & cook at a degree of 400 f till it's crispy for around 15 mins; shake the chickpeas timely while cooking.

4. Place the chickpeas in a tub. Sprinkle it with cilantro, Aleppo pepper and salt; blend to coat.

150. 11. Air fry shrimp spring rolls with sweet chili sauce.

Cook time: 20 mins

Serving: 4

Difficulty: easy

Ingredients:

- 1 cup of matchstick carrots
- 8 (8" square) wrappers of spring roll
- 2 1/2 tbsp. of divided sesame oil
- 4 ounces of peeled, deveined and chopped raw shrimp
- 1/2 cup of chili sauce (sweet)
- 1 cup of (red) bell pepper julienne-cut

- 2 tsp. of fish sauce
- 3/4 cup snow peas julienne-cut
- 2 cups of cabbage, pre-shredded
- 1/4 tsp. of red pepper, crushed
- 1 tbsp. of lime juice (fresh)
- 1/4 cup of fresh cilantro (chopped)

Instructions:

1. In a large pan, heat around 1 1/2 tsp. of oil until softly smoked. Add carrots, bell pepper and cabbage; Cook, stirring constantly, for 1 to 1 1/2 minutes, until finely wilted. Place it on a baking tray; cool for 5 minutes.

2. In a wide tub, place the mixture of cabbage, snow peas, cilantro, fish sauce, red pepper, shrimp and lime juice; toss to blend.

3. Put the wrappers of spring roll on the surface with a corner that is facing you. Add a filling of 1/4 cup in the middle of every wrapper of spring roll, extending from left-hand side to right in a three-inch wide strip.

4. Fold each wrapper's bottom corner over the filling, stuffing the corner tip under the filling. Fold the corners left & right over the filling. Brush the remaining corner softly with water; roll closely against the remaining corner; press gently to cover. Use 2 teaspoons of the remaining oil to rub the spring rolls.

5. Inside the basket of air fryer, put four spring rolls & cook at a degree of 390 f till it's golden, for 6 - 7 minutes, rotating the spring rolls every 5 minutes. Repeat with the leftover spring rolls. Use chili sauce to serve.

Chapter 5: Dessert recipes

151. 1. Air fryer mores

Cook time: 2 mins

Serving: 2 people

Difficulty: easy

Ingredients:

- 1 big marshmallow
- 2 graham crackers split in half
- 2 square, fine quality chocolate

Instructions:

1. Preheat the air fryer at a degree of 330 f.

2. When preheating, break 2 graham crackers into two to form four squares. Cut 1 big marshmallow into half evenly so that one side can be sticky.

3. Add every half of your marshmallow in a square of one graham cracker & push downwards to stick the marshmallow with graham cracker. You must now have two marshmallows coated with graham crackers & two regular graham crackers.

4. In one layer, put two graham crackers and marshmallows inside your air fryer & cook for about 2 minutes till you can see the marshmallow becoming toasted slightly.

5. Remove immediately and completely and add 1 chocolate square to the toasted marshmallow. Add the rest of the squares of the graham cracker and press down. Enjoy instantly.

152. 2. Easy air fryer brownies

Cook time: 15 mins

Serving: 4 people

Difficulty: easy

Ingredients:

- 2 large eggs
- ½ cup flour for all-purpose
- ¼ cup melted unsalted butter
- 6 tbsp. of cocoa powder, unsweetened
- ¼ tsp. of baking powder
- ¾ cup of sugar
- ½ tsp. of vanilla extract
- 1 tbsp. of vegetable oil
- ¼ tsp. of salt

Instructions:

1. Get the 7-inch baking tray ready by gently greasing it with butter on all the sides and even the bottom. Put it aside

2. Preheat the air fryer by adjusting its temperature to a degree of 330 f & leaving it for around 5 minutes as you cook the brownie batter.

3. Add baking powder, cocoa powder, vanilla extract, flour for all-purpose, butter, vegetable oil, salt, eggs and sugar in a big tub & mix it unless well combined.

4. Add up all these for the preparation of the baking pan & clean the top.

5. Put it inside the air fryer & bake it for about 15 minutes or as long as a toothpick can be entered and comes out easily from the center.

6. Take it out and make it cool in the tray until you remove and cut.

153. 3. Easy air fryer churros

Cook time: 5 mins

Serving: 4 people

Difficulty: easy

Ingredients:

- 1 tbsp. of sugar
- Sifted powdered sugar & cinnamon or cinnamon sugar

- 1 cup (about 250ml) water
- 4 eggs
- ½ cup (113g) butter
- ¼ tsp. salt
- 1 cup (120g) all-purpose flour

Instructions:

1. Mix the ingredients bringing them to boil while stirring continuously.
2. Add flour & start mixing properly. Take it out from the heat & mix it till it gets smooth & the dough can be taken out from the pan easily.
3. Add one egg at one time and stir it until it gets smooth. Set it to cool.
4. Preheat your air fryer degree of 400 for 200 c.
5. Cover your bag of cake decorations with dough & add a star tip of 1/2 inch.
6. Make sticks which are having a length of 3 to 4 inches by moving your dough out from the bag in paper (parchment). You can now switch it inside your air fryer if you are ready to do so. If it is hard to handle the dough, put it inside the refrigerator for around 30 minutes.
7. Use cooking spray or coconut oil to spray the tray or the basket of your air fryer.
8. Add around 8 to 10 churros in a tray or inside the basket of the air fryer. Spray with oil.
9. Cook for 5 minutes at a degree of 400 for 200 c.

10. Until finished and when still hot, rill in regular sugar, cinnamon or sugar mixture.

11. Roll in the cinnamon-sugar blend, cinnamon or normal sugar until finished and when still high.

154. 4. Air fryer sweet apples

Cook time: 8 mins

Serving: 4 people

Difficulty: easy

Ingredients:

- ¼ cup of white sugar
- ⅓ Cup of water
- ¼ cup of brown sugar
- ½ tsp. of ground cinnamon
- 6 apples diced and cored
- ¼ tsp. of pumpkin pie spice

- ¼ tsp. of ground cloves

Instructions:

1. Put all the ingredients in a bowl that is oven safe & combine it with water and seasonings. Put the bowl inside the basket, oven tray or even in the toaster of an air fryer.

2. Air fry the mixture of apples at a degree of 350 f for around 6 minutes. Mix the apples & cook them for an extra 2 minutes. Serve it hot and enjoy.

155. 5. Air fryer pear crisp for two

Cook time: 20 mins

Serving: 2

Difficulty: easy

Ingredients:

- ¾ tsp. of divided ground cinnamon
- 1 tbsp. of softened salted butter
- 1 tsp. of lemon juice
- 2 pears. Peeled, diced and cored
- 1 tbsp. of flour for all-purpose
- 2 tbsp. of quick-cooking oats
- 1 tbsp. of brown sugar

Instructions:

1. Your air fryer should be preheated at a degree of 360 f (180 c).

2. Mix lemon juice, 1/4 tsp. Cinnamon and pears in a bowl. Turn for coating and then split the mixture into 2 ramekins.

3. Combine brown sugar, oats, leftover cinnamon and flour in the tub. Using your fork to blend in the melted butter until the mixture is mushy. Sprinkle the pears.

4. Put your ramekins inside the basket of an air fryer & cook till the pears become bubbling and soft for around 18 - 20 minutes.

156. 6. Keto chocolate cake – air fryer recipe

Cook time: 10 mins

Serving: 6 people

Difficulty: easy

Ingredients:

- 1 tsp. of vanilla extract
- 1/2 cup of powdered Swerve
- 1/3 cup of cocoa powder unsweetened
- 1/4 tsp. of salt
- 1 & 1/2 cups of almond flour
- 2 large eggs
- 1/3 cups of almond milk, unsweetened

- 1 tsp. of baking powder

Instructions:

1. In a big mixing tub, mix every ingredient until they all are well mixed.

2. Butter or spray your desired baking dish. We used bunt tins in mini size, but you can even get a 6-inch cake pan in the baskets of the air fryer.

3. Scoop batter equally inside your baking dish or dishes.

4. Set the temperature of the air fryer to a degree of 350 f & set a 10-minute timer. Your cake will be ready when the toothpick you entered comes out clear and clean.

Conclusion:

The air fryer seems to be a wonderful appliance that will assist you with maintaining your diet. You will also enjoy the flavor despite eating high amounts of oil if you prefer deep-fried food.

Using a limited quantity of oil, you will enjoy crunchy & crispy food without the additional adverse risk, which tastes exactly like fried food. Besides, the system is safe & easy to use. All you must do is choose the ingredients needed, and there will be nutritious food available for your family.

An air fryer could be something which must be considered if a person is attempting to eat a diet having a lower-fat diet, access to using the system to prepare a range of foods, & want trouble cooking experience.

CPSIA information can be obtained
at www.ICGtesting.com
Printed in the USA
LVHW060102060322
712726LV00006B/163